D1284710

Best Easy Day Hikes
Milwaukee

Help Us Keep This Guide Up to Date

Every effort has been made by the author and editors to make this guide as accurate and useful as possible. However, many things can change after a guide is published—trails are rerouted, regulations change, facilities come under new management, etc.

We would love to hear from you concerning your experiences with this guide and how you feel it could be improved and kept up to date. While we may not be able to respond to all comments and suggestions, we'll take them to heart and we'll also make certain to share them with the author. Please send your comments and suggestions to the following address:

> Globe Pequot Press
> Reader Response/Editorial Department
> P.O. Box 480
> Guilford, CT 06437

Or you may e-mail us at:

> editorial@GlobePequot.com

Thanks for your input, and happy trails!

Best Easy Day Hikes Series

Best Easy Day Hikes
Milwaukee

Kevin Revolinski

FALCONGUIDES

GUILFORD, CONNECTICUT
HELENA, MONTANA
AN IMPRINT OF GLOBE PEQUOT PRESS

FALCONGUIDES®

Copyright © 2010 by Morris Book Publishing, LLC

FalconGuides is an imprint of Globe Pequot Press.
Falcon, FalconGuides, and Outfit Your Mind are registered trademarks
of Morris Book Publishing, LLC.

TOPO! Explorer software and SuperQuad source maps courtesy of
National Geographic Maps. For information about TOPO! Explorer,
TOPO!, and Nat Geo Maps products, go to www.topo.com or www
.natgeomaps.com.

Maps by Off Route Inc. © Morris Book Publishing, LLC

Library of Congress Cataloging-in-Publication Data is available on file.

ISBN 978-0-7627-5749-7

Printed in the United States of America

10 9 8 7 6 5 4 3 2 1

Contents

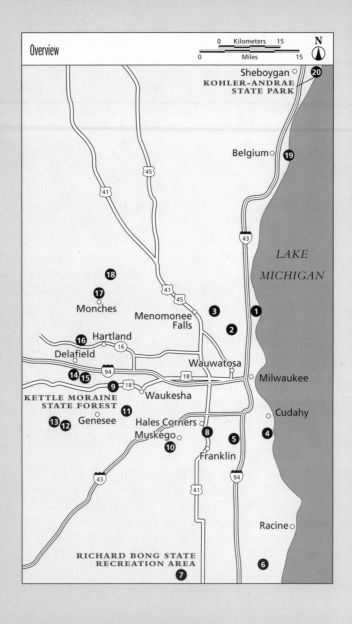

Overview

0 Kilometers 15
0 Miles 15

N

Sheboygan
KOHLER-ANDRAE
STATE PARK

Belgium

LAKE
MICHIGAN

Monches

Menomonee
Falls

Hartland

Delafield

Wauwatosa

Milwaukee

KETTLE MORAINE
STATE FOREST

Waukesha

Cudahy

Genesee

Hales Corners

Muskego

Franklin

RICHARD BONG STATE
RECREATION AREA

Racine

Acknowledgments

A hearty thanks to the various park managers and personnel who helped me keep this guidebook accurate and suggested better routes than the ones I had in mind. I remain a big fan of all the people at the Ice Age Trail Alliance and the trail that gives them their name and purpose. Get out there and support it!

Once again I am forever grateful to the Friends' Hotel Network, especially Erica Chiarkas, Veronica and Alexandra, and Mark Dimeo. A big thanks for a trail drop-off (not to mention a great Turkish dinner!) goes out to Tom and Bezmi Kranick. My old pal Bob Wilson kept me company on a trail, as did the lovely Miss Peung, who did the same for a previous book.

Peung, you *know* this book is for you, right?

Introduction

When you think Milwaukee, the first thing you think of is
. . . well, beer. I might be foolish to think hiking would be
up there near the top of the list, but well it should be. This
major metropolitan area spreads out from its perch on the
shores of Lake Michigan, but good city, county, and state
park systems have preserved green spaces within its limits—
some natural Wisconsin beauty for the urbanites. And just
outside the metro area's reaches lies a trekker's playground
crafted by glaciers over 12,000 years ago.

Much of the land here, in fact, has the MADE IN THE ICE
AGE label on it. The lovely dunes at Kohler-Andrae State
Park are the product of the carving out of Lake Michigan
and the wave action of a giant glacial lake left behind. As the
waters retreated, the dunes were built by the winds.

Parks within the Kettle Moraine State Forest show
a variety of dramatic formations left behind by the last
advance of the ice sheets. The towering kame at Lapham
Peak Park grants views into other counties. I've included
the easier hikes from those areas but these are merely suggestions. You'll find other options—especially in the Kettle
Moraine—for more challenging treks, and Wisconsin's own
Ice Age National Scenic Trail provides a rustic footpath
roughly along the last glacier's farthest reach.

Wildflowers are abundant in Wisconsin and the colors
of the landscape change from spring to summer and into
fall, when the autumnal fires set the hardwood forests ablaze
with red, orange, yellow, and gold. And hiking is not lim-
ited to the warmer seasons either. The Schlitz Audubon
Nature Center offers a tour of unique ice formations from

waters blown in off Lake Michigan, and several other parks offer trails for hiking and snowshoeing.

Whether you are looking for a quick stroll through the city's lakeside Grant Park or a day's hiking along the Ice Age National Scenic Trail, this book can get you there.

The Nature of Milwaukee

Milwaukee's hiking grounds range from wide mowed park paths to rustic footpaths marked by rocks and tree roots climbing over the rugged ridges. Hikes in this guide offer a little bit of each and everything in between. While by definition a best easy day hike is not strenuous and generally poses little danger to the traveler, knowing a few details about the nature of the Milwaukee area will enhance your explorations.

Weather

Spring can start in March or May, depending on the whims of Wisconsin weather. But in general you can expect temperatures to get above freezing in March and stay there by April. In April and May temperatures in the 50s, 60s, and even 70s can be expected. Mosquitoes start coming out later in May—or if you're lucky, June.

Summer temperatures can range from 60s and 70s in June up to 80s and 90s in July and August. But don't be surprised if it's 85 degrees one day and 65 degrees the next day—or even a couple hours later. Mosquitoes and summer go hand in hand, I'm afraid. Watch for thunderstorms or the occasional windstorm or tornado.

Fall brings amazing colors starting in late September and perhaps hanging on past Halloween. Some 70- and

80-degree heat can linger through September, but generally temperatures are mild and the mosquitoes have gone for the year.

Winter means snow. This does not, however, mean the end of the hiking season. Most trails are still open in the winter and snowshoe enthusiasts are happy. However, watch for trails that are closed to hikers when cross-country skiing is possible. Groomed trails as a rule prohibit hiking.

Critters
There's not much in the way of dangerous wildlife around Milwaukee. Don't find yourself on the business end of a skunk. You'll encounter mostly benign, sweet creatures on these trails, such as deer, squirrels, rabbits, wild turkeys, and a variety of songbirds and shorebirds. More rarely seen (during the daylight hours especially) are coyotes, raccoons, and opossums. Deer in some of the parks are remarkably tame, and may linger on or close to the trail as you approach.

One potential critter risk comes from the smallest of the lot: the tick and the mosquito. Lyme disease and West Nile virus can be transmitted through their bites. Protect yourself with light-colored clothing and good insect repellent.

Also, if you decide to incorporate some camping into your hikes, please do not move firewood from site to site: Wisconsin forests are at risk from the emerald ash borer.

Be Prepared

Hiking in the Milwaukee area is generally safe. Still, hikers should be prepared, whether they are out for a short stroll along Lake Michigan or venturing onto the secluded Ice Age National Scenic Trail. Some specific advice:

- Know the basics of first aid, including how to treat bleeding, bites and stings, and fractures, strains, or sprains. Pack a first-aid kit on each excursion.

- Bring insect repellent. Mosquitoes are often referred to as the state bird in Wisconsin and depending on weather conditions, such as wind and recent rainfall, they can be quite a nuisance.

- Familiarize yourself with the symptoms of heat exhaustion and heat stroke. Heat exhaustion symptoms include heavy sweating, muscle cramps, headache, dizziness, and fainting. Should you or any of your hiking party exhibit any of these symptoms, cool the victim down immediately by rehydrating and getting him or her to an air-conditioned location. Cold showers also help reduce body temperature. Heat stroke is much more serious: The victim may lose consciousness and the skin is hot and dry to the touch. In this event, call 911 immediately.

- Regardless of the weather, your body needs a lot of water while hiking. A full 32-ounce bottle is the minimum for these short hikes, but more is always better. Bring a full water bottle, whether water is available along the trail or not.

- Don't drink from streams, rivers, creeks, or lakes without treating or filtering the water first. Waterways and water bodies may host a variety of contaminants, including giardia, which can cause serious intestinal unrest.

- Prepare for extremes of both heat and cold by dressing in layers.

- Carry a backpack in which you can store extra clothing, ample drinking water and food, and whatever goodies, like guidebooks, cameras, and binoculars, you might want.

- Some area trails have cell phone coverage. Bring your device, but make sure you've turned it off or got it on the vibrate setting while hiking. Nothing like a "wake the dead"-loud ring to startle every creature, including fellow hikers.

- Keep children under careful watch. Hazards along some of the trails include poison oak, poison sumac, poison ivy, stinging nettles, wild parsnip, uneven footing, and steep slopes or drop-offs; make sure children don't stray from the designated route. Children should carry a plastic whistle; if they become lost, they should stay in one place and blow the whistle to summon help.

Zero Impact

Trails in the Milwaukee area are heavily used year-round. We, as trail users and advocates, must be especially vigilant to make sure our passage leaves no lasting mark. Here are some basic guidelines for preserving trails in the region:

- Pack out all your own trash, including biodegradable items like orange peels. You might also pack out garbage left by less considerate hikers.

- Don't approach or feed any wild creatures—the ground squirrel eyeing your snack food is best able to survive if it remains self-reliant.

- Don't pick wildflowers or gather rocks, antlers, feathers, and other treasures along the trail. Removing these items will only take away from the next hiker's experience.

- Avoid damaging trailside soils and plants by remaining on the established route. This is also a good rule of thumb for avoiding various irritating plants such as poison ivy or wild parsnip, common regional trailside irritants.
- Don't cut switchbacks, which can promote erosion.
- Be courteous by not making loud noises while hiking.
- Many of these trails are multiuse, which means you'll share them with other hikers, trail runners, mountain bikers, and equestrians. Familiarize yourself with the proper trail etiquette, yielding the trail when appropriate.
- Use outhouses at trailheads or along the trail.

Milwaukee Area Boundaries and Corridors

For the purposes of this guide, best easy day hikes are within a one-hour drive from downtown Milwaukee. The hikes reach into Milwaukee, Kenosha, Racine, Ozaukee, Waukesha, Washington, and Sheboygan counties, and into satellite cities including Wauwatosa, Cudahy, Muskego, Hales Corners, and Franklin.

Two major interstates converge in Milwaukee. Directions to trailheads are given from these arteries. They include I-94 (west to Madison, and east [in reality, south] to Chicago) and I-43 (north to Green Bay/Sheboygan, and south to Beloit).

Land Management

The following government and private organizations manage most of the public lands described in this guide, and can provide further information on these hikes and other trails in their service areas.

- Ice Age Trail Alliance, 2110 Main St., Cross Plains, 53528; (800) 227-0046; www.iceagetrail.org. The Web site has information about local alliance chapters, volunteering, and directions to other trail segments.

- Milwaukee County Park System, 9480 Watertown Plank Rd., Wauwatosa, 53226; (414) 257-7275; www.countyparks.com. The park office is open weekdays from 8 a.m. to 5 p.m.

- Waukesha County Department of Parks and Land Use, Waukesha County Courthouse, 515 West Moreland Blvd., Waukesha, 53188; (262) 548-7790; www.waukeshacountyparks.com; dwalbert@waukeshacounty.gov. The park office is open weekdays from 8 a.m. to 4:30 p.m.

- Wisconsin State Parks, Department of Natural Resources, 101 S. Webster St. (P.O. Box 7921), Madison, 53707; (608) 266-2181; www.dnr.state.wi.us; wiparks@wisconsin.gov. A complete listing of state parks is available on the Web site, along with park brochures and maps.

Public Transportation

The Milwaukee County Transit System offers bus service throughout the greater Milwaukee metropolitan area. Contact information is 1942 North 17th St., Milwaukee, 53205; (414) 344-6711; www.ridemcts.com. Office hours are from 6 a.m. to 7 p.m., Monday through Friday; and from 8:30 a.m. to 4:30 p.m. on Saturday, Sunday, and holidays.

How to Use This Guide

This guide is designed to be simple and easy to use. Each hike is described with a map and summary information that delivers the trail's vital statistics including length, difficulty, fees and permits, park hours, canine compatibility, and trail contacts. Directions to the trailhead are also provided, along with a general description of what you'll see along the way. A detailed route finder (Miles and Directions) sets forth mileages between significant landmarks along the trail.

Hike Selection

This guide describes trails that are accessible to every hiker, whether visiting from out of town or someone lucky enough to live in Milwaukee. The hikes are no longer than 7 miles round-trip, and some are considerably shorter. They range in difficulty from flat excursions perfect for a family outing to more challenging treks along the Ice Age National Scenic Trail. While these trails are among the best, keep in mind that nearby trails, often in the same park or preserve, may offer options better suited to your needs. I've tried to space hikes throughout the Milwaukee area, so wherever your starting point may be, you'll find a great easy day hike nearby.

Difficulty Ratings

These are all easy hikes, but easy is a relative term. To aid in the selection of a hike that suits particular needs and abilities, each hike is still rated easy, moderate, or more challenging, with additional comments to indicate what merited that rating. Bear in mind that even the most challenging routes can be made easier by hiking within your limits and taking rests when you need them.

- **Easy** hikes are generally short and flat, taking no longer than an hour to complete.

- **Moderate** hikes involve increased distance and relatively mild changes in elevation, and will take one to two hours to complete.

- **More challenging** hikes feature some steep stretches, greater distances, and generally take longer than two hours to complete.

These are completely subjective ratings—consider that what you think is easy is entirely dependent on your level of fitness and the adequacy of your gear (primarily shoes). If you are hiking with a group, you should select a hike with a rating that's appropriate for the least fit and prepared in your party.

Approximate hiking times are based on the assumption that on flat ground, most walkers average two miles per hour. Adjust that rate by the steepness of the terrain and your level of fitness (subtract time if you're an aerobic animal and add time if you're hiking with kids), and you have a ballpark hiking duration. Be sure to add more time if you plan to picnic or take part in other activities like bird watching or photography.

Trail Finder

Best Hikes for River Lovers

Best Hikes for Lake Michigan Lovers

Best Hikes for Children

Best Hikes for Dogs

Best Hikes for Great Views

Map Legend

94	Interstate Highway
18	U.S. Highway
32	State Highway
═══	Local Road
▬▬▬	Featured Trail
- - -	Trail
────	Paved Trail
┝┼┼┼┥	Railroad
～～	River/Creek
⬭	Body of Water
⸜⸝	Marsh/Wetland
⊟	Bench
⫼⫼⫼	Boardwalk
⌣	Bridge
▲	Camping
❓	Information Center
🅿	Parking
🅰	Picnic Area
■	Point of Interest/Structure
🚻	Restroom
ơ	Spring
▯	Tower
○	Town
11	Trailhead
🢐	Viewpoint/Overlook
⬛	Water

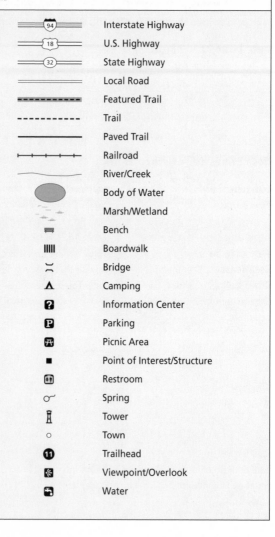

1 Schlitz Audubon Nature Center Trails

Just a fifteen-minute drive from downtown Milwaukee, this lakeside nature center offers easy hikes through a rich preserve, all centered around an outstanding education facility. Fun for all ages, the center also offers organized hikes and other events for nature lovers.

Distance: 3.1-mile circuit
Approximate hiking time: 1.5 to 2 hours
Difficulty: Easy
Trail surface: Cedar chips, packed dirt, and grass, plus some asphalt on wheelchair-accessible trails
Best seasons: Year-round
Other trail users: None
Canine compatibility: Dogs not permitted
Fees and permits: An entrance fee is charged.

Schedule: Open daily from 9 a.m. to 5 p.m.
Maps: USGS Thiensville
Trail contact: Schlitz Audubon Nature Center, 1111 East Brown Deer Rd., Milwaukee 53217; (414) 352-2880; www.sanc.org
Other: Winter hiking is quite popular due to frozen lake formations. The nature center houses interactive exhibits and an auditorium, and hosts frequent classes, presentations, and interpretive hikes.

Finding the trailhead: Take I-43 north to WI 32/East Brown Deer Road. Head east toward the lake. When the highway follows a curve to the right, take the second left to stay on Brown Deer Road. Follow this to its end; the entrance to the nature center is on the right (south). Follow the park road to the nature center parking lots. Restrooms and a shelter are near the trailhead, which is at the end of the small parking lot just beyond the entrance booth. GPS: N43 10.42' / W87 53.07'

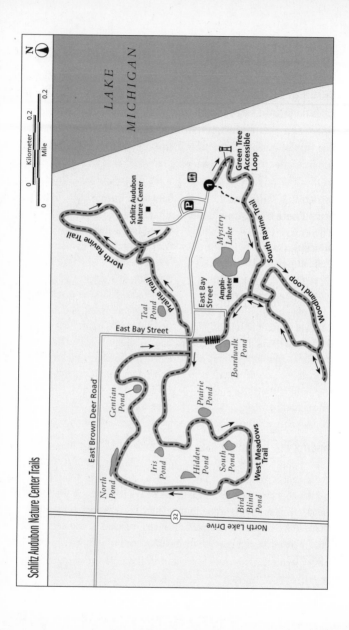

Schlitz Audubon Nature Center Trails

LAKE MICHIGAN

N

Kilometer
0   0.2
0   0.2
Mile

Schlitz Audubon Nature Center

North Ravine Trail

Prairie Trail

Teal Pond

East Bay Street

East Brown Deer Road

Gentian Pond

North Pond

Iris Pond

Hidden Pond

Prairie Pond

South Pond

Bird Blind Pond

West Meadows Trail

North Lake Drive

32

Boardwalk Pond

Amphitheater

Mystery Lake

East Bay Street

P

1

Green Tree Accessible Loop

South Ravine Trail

Woodland Loop

The Hike

This land was where the Schlitz Brewery once grazed the horses that pulled their beer wagons. It's now the home of an Audubon nature center that offers a variety of education programs and a wealth of information. The 185-acre property has six looped hiking trails linked by connecting trails and totaling about 5 miles. The hike laid out here makes a circuit of them. Pay your park entrance fee at the visitor center.

Look for the entry booth at the beginning of the parking lots. The lot just past the booth is closest to the trailhead. The hike begins on the Green Tree accessible asphalt loop trail. The trail joins the lot on the right (south), and you can go left or right. Start down the trail to the left (southeast) and you will immediately come to the observation tower. Continue to a juncture where the asphalt goes right (north), but a rustic footpath heads left (west). Take the rustic path and you are on the 0.65-mile South Ravine Trail.

Stay straight, passing a cutoff to the right (north) and you'll come to steps on your left leading down into a ravine and up the other side. This is the start of the 0.4-mile Woodland Loop.

At the end of the Woodland Loop, take the spur to Solitude Marsh and back. Return to the Woodland Loop, which ends at the next juncture, just a few steps farther along the South Ravine Trail. Here you can either go right (east), returning to the trailhead, or left (west) on a connector trail. Follow the connector across a park service road before arriving at a boardwalk over a pond. Cross this and continue north to the 1.3-mile West Meadows Trail, which offers several places to observe wildlife around some ponds. A cutoff trail halves the distance of its loop.

Upon completing the loop, cross the park entrance road to connect to the Prairie and North Ravine Trails, a sort of figure eight totaling 0.8 mile. You can follow them as one big loop by taking the left (north) branch at the first two junctures and then returning to the nature center after the turnaround at the northernmost point.

If you want to extend this hike a bit, the 0.8-mile Lake Terrace Trail has a connector trail from the North Ravine Trail. You can expect views of the lake and beach and some sandy trail surface on this trail.

Miles and Directions

0.0 Start on the paved Green Tree accessible trail.

0.4 Take the steps to the Woodland Loop.

1.0 Cross the boardwalk over the pond.

1.1 Join the West Meadows Trail.

2.0 Arrive at North Pond.

2.4 Begin the Prairie Trail.

2.7 Meet the North Ravine Trail.

3.1 Arrive back at nature center parking lot.

2 Havenwoods State Forest

Though there are indeed rich woods within the park, the prairie flowers may steal the show and the wetlands offer even more variety. You may forget you are in the city as you walk down what feels like a classic country road.

Distance: 2.5-mile circuit

Approximate hiking time: 1 to 1.5 hours

Difficulty: Easy

Trail surface: Crushed limestone, grass, some asphalt

Best seasons: Late spring, summer, early fall

Other trail users: Bicycles on limestone and asphalt portions

Canine compatibility: Leashed dogs permitted on designated trails

Fees and permits: None required

Schedule: Open from 6 a.m. to 8 p.m. daily

Maps: USGS Thiensville and Milwaukee; park map available at the Havenwoods Environmental Awareness Center

Trail contacts: Havenwoods State Forest, 6141 N. Hopkins St.; Milwaukee 53209; (414) 527-0232; www.dnr.state.wi.us/org/land/parks/specific/havenwoods/; www.friendsofhavenwoods.org

Special considerations: Be careful of wild parsnip, the oils of which can react with the skin, causing a chemical burn activated by sunlight.

Other: The Havenwoods Environmental Awareness Center is open from 7:45 a.m. to 4:30 p.m. Mon through Fri, and from 9 a.m. to noon on Sat. It offers a variety of printed materials, including wildlife checklists, a seasonal program calendar, and Wisconsin Explorer activity books for kids. Accessible restrooms are inside the building.

Finding the trailhead: From I-43 take Silver Spring Drive west to North Sherman Boulevard. Go right (north) to Douglas Avenue. Go west 1 block, where the street ends at the entrance to the park. The trailhead and kiosk are at the southwest corner of the parking lot right next to the education center. GPS: N43 07.71' / W87 58.18'

The Hike

This 237-acre state forest is right inside the city limits. Homesteaders occupied this space in the nineteenth century, but then the county's correctional facility took over. Army barracks and a Nike missile site also used the space before it became a preserve. The trails show abundant wildflowers in the prairie and woodland areas, and some restored wetlands round out the mix.

The trail described here is primarily crushed limestone, with a short stretch of asphalt. The other segments are mowed grass, which can hold a lot of dew in the mornings. Dogs are allowed on 8-foot leashes on the limestone path; consult the park map, found at the kiosk or education center, for other trails in the park that allow pets.

A few paces from the kiosk the trail splits: Follow the limestone trail that heads straight south. You will pass several optional spur trails into the woods to your left (east). Just after the first spur trail on your right (west), follow the limestone loop trail into the woods on your left (east). This will cross an intermittent creek twice before returning you to the main track.

Continuing (southwest) on the main trail you will reach the property boundary and a map board. The path looks like a country road and heads right (northwest), paralleling the railroad tracks through the brush on your left (southwest).

Cross Lincoln Creek and a grassy trail on the right (north), and keep straight, passing the next limestone path on your right. The main trail loops right (east) and brings you to a juncture. The right branch would complete a loop

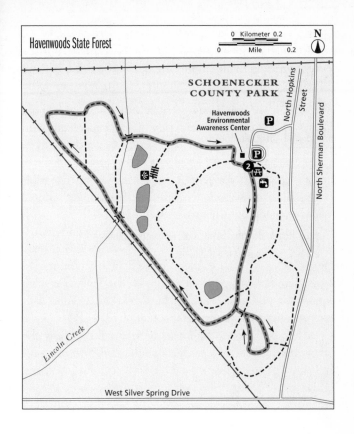

0   Kilometer   0.2

0   Mile   0.2

N

SCHOENECKER
COUNTY PARK

North Hopkins
Street

Havenwoods
Environmental
Awareness Center

P

P

2

North Sherman Boulevard

Lincoln Creek

West Silver Spring Drive

and take you back to the railroad tracks; instead take the grassy trail to the left (northeast). Climb a short hill and cross the creek on a long metal bridge. The next trail on your right (south) leads down to a boardwalk and platform overlooking one of the four ponds in the park. *Dogs are not allowed on this portion of the trail or in any other part of the wetlands.*

Backtrack from the pond out to the main trail, where it becomes an asphalt service road. Follow the road to the education center and loop to the right behind the building to return to the trailhead, or simply walk straight out on the road to the parking lot.

Miles and Directions

- **0.0** Start from the trail kiosk on the limestone path.
- **0.4** Explore the woodland loop.
- **1.2** Cross Lincoln Creek.
- **1.9** Cross a long metal bridge.
- **2.1** Reach the boardwalk and observation platform.
- **2.5** Arrive back at the trailhead.

3 Kohl Park Hiking Trail

An easy escape from the city, this trail is short and sweet, buried in a hardwood forest. Now a national recreation trail, the hike is getting more attention. The fall colors are a must-see.

Distance: 1.4-mile lollipop
Approximate hiking time: 45 minutes
Difficulty: Easy
Trail surface: Cedar chips, grass, packed dirt
Best seasons: Spring, summer, fall
Other trail users: None
Canine compatibility: Leashed dogs permitted

Fees and permits: No fees or permits required
Schedule: Open daily, sunrise until 10 p.m.
Maps: USGS Menomonee Falls
Trail contact: Milwaukee County Park System, 9480 Watertown Plank Rd., Wauwatosa 53226; (414) 257-7275; www.county parks.com

Finding the trailhead: From I-43, take Brown Deer Road/WI 100 west to 91st Street. Go right (north) 0.5 mile to Fairy Chasm Drive and turn right (east). Find the trailhead at 0.1 mile along Fairy Chasm Drive on the left (north) side of the street. Parking is roadside. GPS: N43 11.11' / W88 01.27'

The Hike

These trails were first laid out in 2006. By 2009 the Kohl Park Hiking Trail had garnered some national attention when it was designated as a national recreation trail. The trail's creation was a collaboration between Milwaukee County, local conservation groups, scouting groups, and

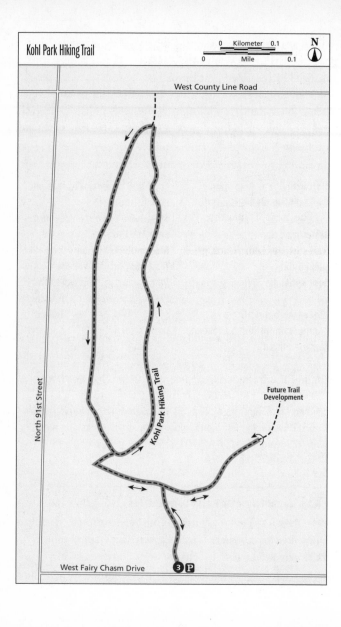

Kohl Park Hiking Trail

West County Line Road

North 91st Street

Kohl Park Hiking Trail

Future Trail
Development

West Fairy Chasm Drive

3 **P**

volunteers. The land preserved here once included a Christmas tree farm, and you can still see an old silo slowly being taken in by the forest and brush.

The trail descends from the roadside into thick woods. At the first juncture go right (east), which is an out-and-back segment that passes along farmland and prairie. When you come back to the first juncture, go left (west), continuing among the hardwoods. At the next juncture a spur trail exits the park onto 91st Street. Continue on the main trail to the right (north).

The next T juncture is the start of the loop. Take the path to the right, passing through woods and some open spaces as the trail heads north. You will find a few benches along the trail.

The next trail junction is with a spur going right (north) out to County Line Road. Stay left and follow the loop as it makes the big turn to the south. You'll pass another spur trail to the road and an old silo on the right (west). Then you come back to where the loop began and backtrack out to the trailhead.

This trail continues to be under development. When you visit, the trail from the out-and-back branch will likely be extended.

Miles and Directions

- **0.0** Start from the trailhead.
- **0.1** Go right (east) at the first juncture.
- **0.4** Return to first juncture.
- **0.9** Pass the exit trail to County Line Road.
- **1.2** Pass an old silo.
- **1.4** Arrive back at the trailhead.

4 Grant Park: Seven Bridges Trail

Enjoy a historic trail system that follows ravines and babbling brooks, creating a network of short paths along the shore of Lake Michigan. You'll find more bridges to cross than the name suggests.

Distance: 2-mile network

Approximate hiking time: 1 to 2 hours

Difficulty: Moderate to difficult due to steepness and surface

Trail surface: Packed dirt and Lannon stone

Best seasons: Spring, summer, fall

Other trail users: None

Canine compatibility: Leashed dogs permitted, but not on the beach

Fees and permits: No fees or permits required

Schedule: Open daily from sunrise to 10 p.m.

Maps: USGS South Milwaukee; map board at the trailhead

Trail contact: Milwaukee County Park System, 9480 Watertown Plank Rd., Wauwatosa 53226; (414) 257-7275; www.county parks.com

Finding the trailhead: From downtown Milwaukee head south on I-94 to exit 319 for CR ZZ/College Avenue. Go east to where the road ends at Lake Drive/WI 32. Go right (south) and travel 2 blocks to the park entrance, Grant Park Drive, on your left (east). The roadside parking lot for the trailhead is on the left (east) at about 0.25 mile. The trailhead is at the map board near the covered bridge. Restrooms and water are near the parking areas. GPS: N42 55.39' / W87 50.89'

The Hike

You may count ten bridges, actually. Kids especially will love this network of trails and its Lannon stone paths and staircases laid out by more than two hundred Civilian Conservation Corps workers back in the 1930s. In the 1990s the Wisconsin Conservation Corps helped restore some of the steps and trails, and since 2006 the Milwaukee Conservation Leadership Corps has worked on conservation and erosion control.

The trails crisscross and meander—but not very far—through the woods along brooks cradled in ravines. It doesn't quite lend itself to loops but the joy here is random exploration, as well as access to the beach where you can see rising cliffs far to the north.

The trailhead is at the map board at the parking area. You can enter to the left (northeast), descending steps to a path that follows the river, or pass across a bridge with a large covered gateway to the right (southeast).

From that initial bridge, take the trail left (east) along the edge at the top of the ravine. You'll see the path on the other side of the stream below. Trails also lead off into the forest and to the next picnic area, or you can follow the ravine-edge trail to where a steep trail descends to a bridge to the other side of the ravine and stream.

On the opposite side of the ravine, take the path to the right (east) if you want to exit to the beach. Otherwise go back upstream and cross a bridge over a smaller brook (where it joins the main branch) to a major trail juncture. At this juncture you can simply return to the trailhead by continuing along the main ravine to the stairs back up to the parking lot. But there is more to explore from this juncture. To the right (north) is the first of three bridges that zigzag over the smaller brook. Trails continue north from here. If you climb the bluff to the right (east) you can find trails that follow the edge of the bluff overlooking the beach.

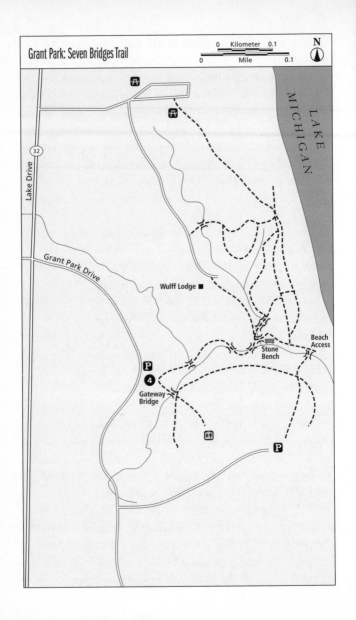

Grant Park: Seven Bridges Trail

0   Kilometer   0.1

0   Mile   0.1

N

LAKE MICHIGAN

Lake Drive

32

Grant Park Drive

Wulff Lodge ■

P

4

Gateway Bridge

Stone Bench

Beach Access

P

Also from the major trail juncture, you can climb a steep staircase up out of the ravine and past Wulff Lodge, named for its former occupant and first superintendent of horticulture for the park system, Frederick Wulff. Near a playground just beyond is a trail to the right (southeast), off the park service road. This crosses yet another bridge to a loop that follows the ravine a bit more. The trails continue north closer to shore, taking you out to picnic areas 8 and 9, where you will find shelters and restrooms.

5 Falk Park

This dog-friendly park south of the city is a tangle of paths in wet woodlands. At the center of its labyrinth is a Minotaur of an oak.

Distance: 1.1-mile loop
Approximate hiking time: 1 hour
Difficulty: Easy to moderate due to trail surface
Trail surface: Cedar chips, packed dirt or mud
Best seasons: Spring, summer, fall
Other trail users: None
Canine compatibility: Leashed dogs permitted

Fees and permits: No fees or permits required
Schedule: Open daily, sunrise until 10 p.m.
Maps: USGS Greendale
Trail contact: Milwaukee County Park System, 9480 Watertown Plank Rd., Wauwatosa 53226; (414) 257-7275; www.county parks.com

Finding the trailhead: From downtown Milwaukee take I-94 east toward Chicago for about 9 miles to exit 320 for West Rawson Avenue/CR BB. Go right (west) for 0.2 miles on West Rawson Avenue and the Falk Park parking lot and pavilion will be on your left (south). The address of the pavilion is 2013 West Rawson Ave. The trailhead is at the back of the lot. GPS: N42 54.94' / W87 56.46'

The Hike

The 216-acre Falk Park is a thick collection of wet woodlands with some intermittent creeks flowing through. For the most part this is a well-shaded hike and you will hear a lot of birds, especially woodpeckers. Many of the trees are beech and maple, but you will also see a fair share of hickory

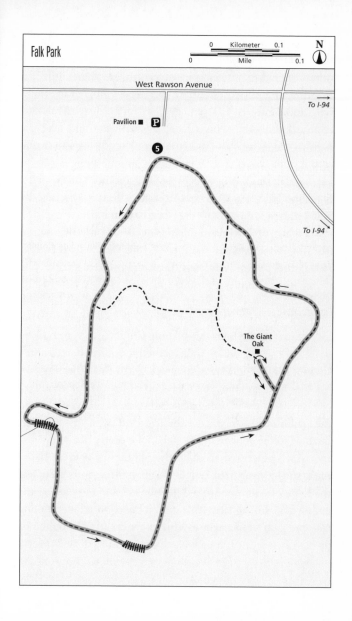

Falk Park

0   Kilometer   0.1

0   Mile   0.1

N

West Rawson Avenue

To I-94 →

Pavilion ■ P

5

To I-94

The Giant
Oak

and oaks. The path is covered with some cedar chips in places, but is simply packed dirt and dead leaves in most others. A few boardwalks cross the lowest points, but if it is spring or a rainy period you can expect a bit of sogginess here and there.

Duck into the woods from the trailhead and take the path to the right at the first juncture. You'll pass a spur trail to the right (west) at 0.15 mile but continue straight (south) on the main trail. A few paces past this another trail connects from the left (east). This cutoff would shorten the hike by half and heads directly to the giant central oak.

Staying on the main trail, however, continue straight (south). Another spur trail at 0.2 mile heads to the right (west) and peters out alongside an intermittent creek. The main trail continues past this spur and crosses two boardwalk footbridges at 0.3 mile. The creek loops under both of them. At 0.5 mile another boardwalk takes you over the lowest part of the hike. At 0.7 mile you'll pass a spur trail on your right (east), which follows the intermittent creek. Stay straight (north) and cross the creek and a small clearing.

The next trail juncture gives you an option you shouldn't pass up. The path to the right (northeast) leads you back to the trailhead. But first, take the left (northwest) path a short distance to the enormous oak tree in the center of a soggy low spot. Two other oaks stand nearby, almost like sentries. Backtrack to the main trail and turn left (northeast) to complete the loop, or continue around the tree's clearing to pick up the cutoff trail. In the latter case, you'll come to a juncture and take the path to the right (north) to get back to the trailhead.

The outside loop of this route is 1.1 miles but a bit of crisscrossing and perhaps using other trails to create a figure-eight path will extend it a bit.

Miles and Directions

0.0 Start by heading south from the parking lot and pavilion.

0.3 Cross two boardwalks.

0.5 Cross the third boardwalk.

0.8 Visit the central oak tree, then backtrack to the main trail and continue left (northeast).

1.1 Arrive back at the trailhead.

6 Petrifying Springs County Park

Take the easy path around this nicely wooded park offering views of the Pike River, and then stop for a picnic in the center of the park or even a round of golf on the park's course.

Distance: 2.7-mile loop

Approximate hiking time: 1 to 1.5 hours

Difficulty: Easy to moderate due to some steepness

Trail surface: Packed dirt, some cedar chips

Best seasons: Spring, summer, and especially fall

Other trail users: None

Canine compatibility: Leashed

dogs permitted

Fees and permits: No fees or permits required

Schedule: Open from 7 a.m. to 10 p.m. daily

Maps: USGS Racine South

Trail contact: Petrifying Springs County Park, 761 Green Bay Rd., Kenosha 53144; (262) 857-1869; www.co.kenosha.wi.us/publicworks/parks/index.html

Finding the trailhead: Take I-94 south to exit 337. Go left (east) on CR KR. Turn right (south) on Green Bay Road/WI 31 and then left (east) on CR A. The park entrance is on the right. GPS: N42 39.25' / W87 52.45'

The Hike

Commonly referred to as "Pets," this 360-acre park and golf course takes its name from springs rich with minerals. The amount of limestone in the water was so great that even acorns or leaves that fell in would get coated with a hard mineral shell as if they were being petrified.

The main loop trail passes through hardwood forest, open areas of the park, and along the golf course. Begin at the parking lot at the park entrance on CR A. Cross the

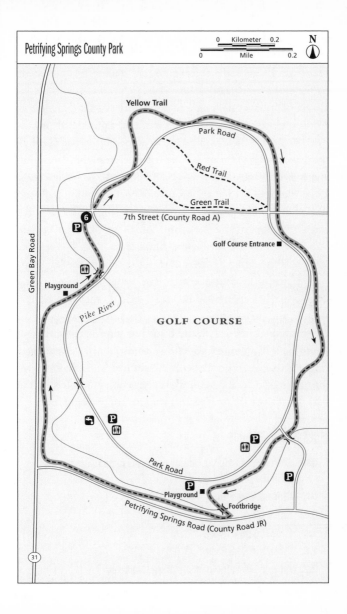

Petrifying Springs County Park

0 Kilometer 0.2
0 Mile 0.2

N

Yellow Trail

Park Road

Red Trail

Green Trail

7th Street (County Road A)

6
P

Golf Course Entrance ■

Green Bay Road

Playground ■

Pike River

GOLF COURSE

P

P

Park Road

P

Playground ■

P

Footbridge

Petrifying Springs Road (County Road JR)

county road where the park road enters the woods to the north. Go to the right (east) side of the road and you will see a map board and a cedar-chip trail leading up at an angle to the right (northeast).

At 0.2 mile you'll come to a juncture with the green trail to the right (southeast); the red trail is straight ahead (northeast). Either of these will take you across the upper curve of the park's loop. Instead go left (north), cross the park road, and follow its edge to where you'll find a trail into the woods. Take the right branch of this to stay on the yellow trail, and stay right again at the next juncture, and the path will curve across the top of the park too. All three of these options reunite back at CR A near the entrance to the golf course.

Cross the county road and seek the trail to the left (east) side of the golf course entry. Pass along the edge of the course and through woods, join the park road for a short stretch, and then follow the Pike River into the picnic areas. Cross the park road with the bridge to your left (south) and at the next playground go left (southeast) and cross the river on a footbridge. The trail climbs as it heads north. Descend into a parking area, pass another playground, and follow the park road over the bridge and back to the parking lot.

Miles and Directions

0.0	Start by crossing the county road and heading northeast from the map board.
0.2	Cross the park road.
0.8	Cross CR A.
1.4	Pass the park bridge.
1.6	Cross the Pike River.
2.7	Arrive back at the parking lot and trailhead.

7 Richard Bong State Recreation Area: Blue Trail

Take a long stroll through one of the area's most popular state park retreats. Trails pass through the largest managed grassland in this corner of the state and it's just awash with wildflowers.

Distance: 4.2-mile loop

Approximate hiking time: 1 to 2 hours

Difficulty: Easy to moderate due to some steepness

Trail surface: Grass and packed dirt that may be quite muddy in spring

Best seasons: Spring, summer, fall

Other trail users: None

Canine compatibility: Leashed dogs permitted

Fees and permits: State park vehicle fee required

Schedule: Open daily from 6 a.m. to 11 p.m.

Maps: USGS Rochester, Union Grove, Silver Lake, Paddock Lake, on Web site and at park office

Trail contact: Richard Bong State Recreation Area; 26313 Burlington Rd., Kansasville 53139; (262) 878-5600; www .dnr.state.wi.us/org/LAND/ parks/specific/bong

Special considerations: Hunting pheasant and waterfowl from lakeside blinds is permitted on the Blue Trail in the fall from 9 a.m. to 2 p.m. The Green Trail is in a nonhunting area. Check the DNR website (dnr.wi.gov) for current hunting season dates. (Dates vary by species of bird and each year may change based upon assessment of population.)

Finding the trailhead: From I-94 near Kenosha, take WI 142 (Burlington Road) west. Cross WI 75 and continue for 0.9 mile to the park entrance on the left (south). From the entrance station take the next road to the left (east) and the trailhead parking lot is on your left. The trailhead for the Blue and Green Trails is at the far (east) end of the parking lot. The park has restrooms and water. GPS: N42 38.05' / W88 07.44'

The Hike

This 4,515-acre state park is named for Wisconsin native and World War II flying ace, Major Richard I. Bong. Activities range from hiking and swimming to model airplane flying and hunting. The trail system collectively totals over 41 miles and hiking trails are color-coded. This is the largest managed grassland in southeastern Wisconsin and if you enjoy wildflowers, this is a hotspot for them. Benches are spread intermittently throughout.

The difference between the Green and Blue Trails, other than length (1.8 and 4.2 miles respectively), is that the Blue has more moderate to strenuous steep sections. These are, however, short stretches of never more than about 75 feet. Additionally the Blue Trail gets its extra length by going all the way around Wolf Lake. The bridle trail crosses at several points, and some spur trails are clearly marked as such. The hiking trails are marked with color-coded posts.

From the parking lot the Blue and Green Trails begin together on a boardwalk through cattails past a couple of observation points. On the other side a section of grass trail begins and crosses the park road to arrive at the first trail juncture. Take the left (northeast) path, following the arrows, which indicate trail colors. You'll pass a sledding hill and some forested portions.

The Blue Trail leaves the Green at 0.9 mile and goes south around the lake, while the Green Trail stays north of the lake and completes a 1.8-mile loop back to the trailhead.

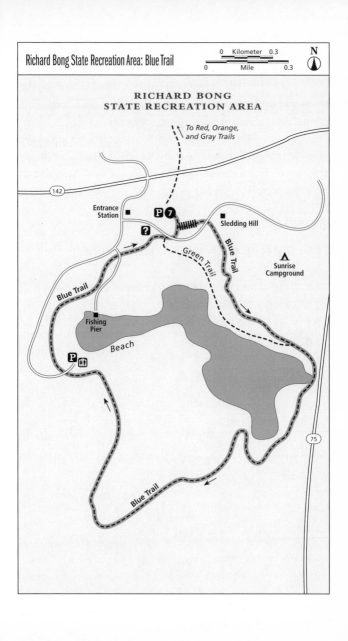

Richard Bong State Recreation Area: Blue Trail

0   Kilometer   0.3
0   Mile   0.3

N

RICHARD BONG
STATE RECREATION AREA

To Red, Orange,
and Gray Trails

142

Entrance
Station

P 7

Sledding Hill

?

Green Trail

Blue Trail

Sunrise
Campground

Blue Trail

Fishing
Pier

Beach

P

75

Blue Trail

Continuing on the Blue Trail, at 2 miles a shaded bench offers a scenic shoreline view of the lake.

The Blue Trail crosses the park roads leading to the beach and fishing pier areas before rejoining the Green Trail for the short distance back to the trailhead.

There are also two self-guided nature trails within the park (dogs not allowed), one of which intersects with the Blue Trail. The Orange, Red, and Gray Trails are north of the highway.

Miles and Directions

0.0 Start by crossing the boardwalk through cattails.

0.3 Pass the sled hill.

0.9 Arrive at the Green Trail split. Continue on the Blue Trail.

2.0 Pass the lakeview bench.

2.5 Pass Orchard Pond on the left (south).

2.8 Cross the beach area road.

3.5 Cross the road to the fishing pier.

4.2 Arrive back at the trailhead.

8 Wehr Nature Center Trails

The wildlife is abundant along this network of trails that combines woodlands and wetlands, prairie and savanna, for a nature lover's perfect package. The center also offers a schedule of guided hikes and events.

Distance: 2.8-mile loop
Approximate hiking time: 1.5 hours
Difficulty: Easy to moderate due to some rough trail and steepness
Trail surface: Cedar chip, packed dirt, some boardwalks
Best seasons: Spring, summer, fall
Other trail users: None
Canine compatibility: Dogs not permitted
Fees and permits: No entry fee but a daily parking fee is charged

Schedule: Trails are open year round from 8 a.m. to dark; the visitor center and parking lot close at 4:30 p.m.
Maps: USGS Hales Corners, posted at the trailhead and available in the nature center
Trail contacts: Wehr Nature Center, 9701 West College Ave., Franklin 53132; (414) 425-8550; www.countyparks.com; www.friendsofwehr.org
Special considerations: Plank walkways in the woods can be very slippery when wet.

Finding the trailhead: From downtown Milwaukee take I-43 south toward Beloit. Exit at WI 100/US 45/108th Street and go south. Take a left on College Avenue, heading east. The park entrance is on the right (south) inside Whitnall Park. Proceed to the parking area. The trailhead is to the left (east) of the nature center, which offers water and restrooms. GPS: N42 55.52' / W88 02.15'

The Hike

Woodland, oak savanna, prairie, and wetland are all neatly packed into this nature park within the larger Whitnall Park. A labyrinth of trails awaits, with an abundance of active wildlife—from songbirds and waterfowl to deer and their fawns—and a variety of wildflowers. There are a number of loop options depending on your interests and time. The route suggested here makes a circuit of the entire natural area, passing through a portion of all loops, but certainly you have the option of lingering in one loop or another.

This is a park worth returning to often. Stop in at the nature center for information about what's to see each time you visit.

The trail begins just to the left (east) of the center, and at the first juncture goes to the right (southwest) along Mallard Lake. You'll pass a boardwalk and observation platform over the water on your left. At the next juncture keep left (south) and the boardwalk begins. You'll cross a second boardwalk before the trail becomes natural surface.

Skirt the edge of a golf course to the right (south), finally joining a crushed stone road. Hike 100 feet and watch left (northwest) for a trail post to follow the trail into the woods again. Come around the lake and pass the waterfall on your left (west). Narrow dirt paths skirt along the river's edge while the main trail stays on a better surface. You'll come out into a mowed area close to the park road and use the street bridge to cross the river. Then keep left (south) along the woods and get back onto the path covered with cedar chips.

Stay left (south), passing a prairie path on the right (west), and then arrive at a four-way juncture. Take the

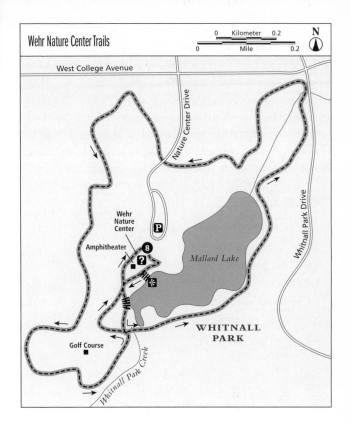

West College Avenue

Nature Center Drive

Whitnall Park Drive

Wehr
Nature
Center

P

Amphitheater

8

?

Mallard Lake

**WHITNALL
PARK**

Golf Course

Whitnall Park Creek

right (west) turn and climb a bit as you cross the prairie, then the park road, and enter into oak savanna. At the first trail juncture here you will take the branch to the right (north). This heads into the woods before looping back across the savanna to the woodland trails.

At the edge of the trees, take the trail to the right (west), and then the next left-leading trail into the woods (heading south). Follow the woodland path to the wetland trails.

Take the next two paths heading right (south, then west), and you will go uphill to the top, where the route turns left (south). Begin a descent to another plank walk. This will connect back to the trail you came in on at Mallard Lake. Go left (west), take the plank walk at the next left, and the path will take you on another boardwalk that loops back to the main trail. Again go left, and take the next left on a trail that will return you to the back side of the nature center, passing the amphitheater along the way.

Miles and Directions

0.0 Start by heading toward Mallard Lake.
0.7 Pass the waterfall.
1.0 Cross the street bridge.
1.4 Cross the park road.
1.8 Enter the woodland trail area.
2.5 Get on the boardwalk on the return path.
2.8 Arrive back at the nature center.

9 Retzer Nature Center Trails

From a meadow overlook scan the horizon for miles around, then descend into one of the few places in this part of the state to observe the type of wetland known as a fen.

Distance: 3-mile circuit

Approximate hiking time: 1.5 hours

Difficulty: Moderate due to steepness

Trail surface: Grass, packed soil, wood chips, some boardwalk

Best seasons: Spring, summer, fall

Other trail users: None

Canine compatibility: Dogs not permitted

Fees and permits: No fees or permits required

Schedule: Open from sunrise to 10 p.m. year-round

Maps: USGS Hartland, map board near trailhead, and maps available in the learning center

Trail contact: Retzer Nature Center, S14 W28167 Madison St., Waukesha 53188; (262) 896-8007; www.waukeshacounty parks.com

Other: The Environmental Learning Center is open daily from 8 a.m. to 4:30 p.m.

Finding the trailhead: Go west on I-94 to Waukesha and take exit 291 for CR TT. Go left (south) to US 18 and turn right (west). Follow US 18 to CR DT and turn left (south). The next left (southeast) is Madison Street, and the nature center entrance is on the right (south). Park in the lot near the learning center. The trailhead is to the left (south) of the building as you approach. Restrooms and water are available inside the Environmental Learning Center. GPS: N43 00.91' / W88 18.68'

The Hike

The Environmental Learning Center and its planetarium make this a great place to take the family. The trails offer a hike through a rather uncommon ecosystem known as a fen, a wetland with an internal flow of water rich with calcium and magnesium. Other parks generally have wheelchair-accessible portions of trails, but Retzer Nature Center also provides braille signs along its 800-foot paved interpretive Adventure Trail.

As you approach the Environmental Learning Center, the trailhead and map board are on the left (south). Follow the asphalt path and you will come to a picnic area under pines. Go left of the picnic area, bearing south on a wood-chip trail marked with color-coded posts. This is the Outer Hiking Loop (green).

The trail immediately leaves the trees and follows wide mowed paths across meadows full of wildflowers. The first juncture is with the Prairie Vista Trail (yellow) on your right (west). Just a few steps down this 0.3-mile loop is an overlook of the prairie and the hills to the south far beyond the park. Continue around the loop.

Return to the Outer Hiking Loop (green trail), and as you crest the hill take a connector trail left (east) to the outside trail (Winter Trail). Follow that down the hill along the edge of the woods to get to the Fen Boardwalk Trail. This 0.75-mile loop passes through unusual wetlands partly on boardwalks, and offers an elevated observation deck. Parts of the trail may be soggy at times. You will pass over a small river on a footbridge as the loop returns to the prairie.

Backtrack up the hill and rejoin the green trail, turning left (west), then left again (southwest) as the path curves

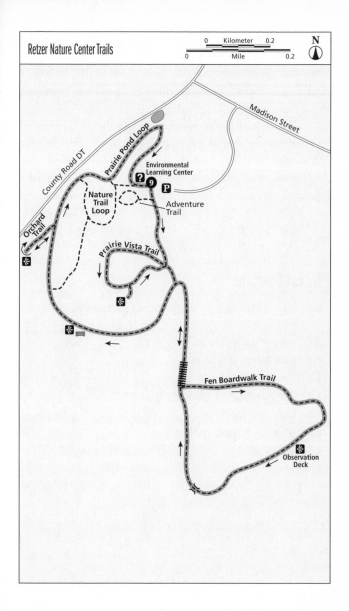

Retzer Nature Center Trails

0   Kilometer   0.2

0   Mile   0.2

N

County Road DT

Madison Street

Prairie Pond Loop

Environmental
Learning Center

?

9

P

Orchard
Trail

Nature
Trail
Loop

Adventure
Trail

Prairie Vista Trail

Fen Boardwalk Trail

Observation
Deck

across the meadow. It will cross the red Winter Trail just before entering into the woods.

In the woods you will find more boardwalks over tiny streams and some moderate climbs. Watch on your left (west) for the purple Orchard Trail; take this 0.3-mile out-and-back spur trail past a barn to an observation point.

Return to the green trail and continue along the several boardwalks. At the next trail juncture, the red Nature Trail Loop joins from the right (south). Take the left (north) path until you come to the blue Prairie Pond Loop trail on your left (north). This path takes you almost 0.3 mile out to a pond, and then back to the learning center and the trailhead.

Miles and Directions

0.0 Start by heading south on the asphalt path past the picnic area.

0.3 Join the Prairie Vista Trail.

0.8 Enter the Fen Boardwalk Trail.

1.2 Stop on the observation deck.

1.8 Return to the green Outer Hiking Loop trail.

2.3 Start the Orchard Trail.

2.7 Arrive at the Prairie Pond Loop.

3.0 Arrive back at the Environmental Learning Center.

10 Muskego Park

The hardwood forest in Muskego Park is the subject of state scientific research, and the park's wetlands give a nice balance to the hike. A sort of open-air museum—or graveyard of the agriculture days—is an interesting distraction along the trail.

Distance: 1.4-mile loop
Approximate hiking time: 30 minutes to 1 hour
Difficulty: Easy
Trail surface: Wood chips, packed dirt
Best seasons: Year-round
Other trail users: Equestrians
Canine compatibility: Leashed dogs permitted; you are required to pick up after your pet

Fees and permits: A daily entrance fee is charged, or you can purchase a yearly vehicle sticker.
Schedule: Open from sunrise to 10 p.m. year-round
Maps: USGS Muskego
Trail contact: Muskego Park, S83 W20370 Janesville Rd., Muskego 53150; (262) 679-0310; www .waukeshacountyparks.com

Finding the trailhead: From Milwaukee take I-43 south toward Beloit. Get off at the CR Y/Racine Avenue exit and go left (south) for 2.4 miles. Turn right (southwest) on CR L/Janesville Road, and the park entrance is 1 mile farther on your right (north). Drive straight into the park to picnic area #4 on your right (east). The trailhead is behind the restrooms and handicap parking space. GPS: N42 53.92' / W88 09.86'

The Hike

Another one of Waukesha County's fine parks, Muskego Park includes a two-acre swimming pond and a twenty-four-site campground. The trees this trail passes through

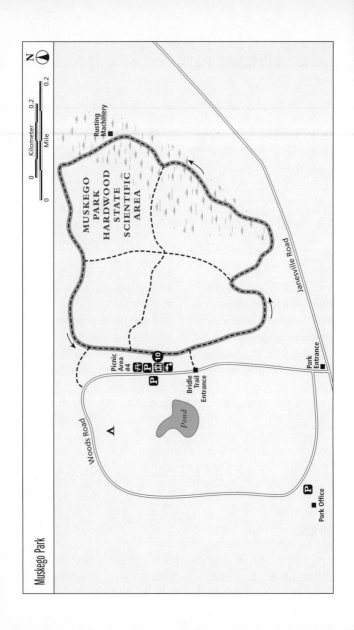

Muskego Park

are part of a sixty-acre hardwood preservation area popu-lated primarily by old-growth white and red oaks but also maples, shagbark hickory, walnut, basswood, and, notably, Kentucky coffee tree and blue ash.

From the trailhead go right (south) on the trail loop. Whereas dog owners are obliged to pick up their compan-ions' droppings, horse riders aren't. Watch your step.

The next trail, coming in on your right (west), is the bridle trail entrance; keep going straight (south). At 0.3 mile you come to a trail juncture. The path straight ahead is actu-ally the cutoff trail, which curves north and goes straight up through the center of the loop, crossing a similar path that bisects the loop from east to west. At this juncture take the right (south) branch to stay on the outer loop trail.

The trail curls around the south end of the park and on your left (north) you will see wetlands with some open water. At 0.6 mile the trail passes right along the edge of the backyards of local residences. Keep along the brush line and continue to where the trail heads back into the woods. After another 0.1 mile you will pass the second cutoff trail on your left (west). Stay right (northeast). Just around the next bend you'll start passing through old, rusting hulks of farm equipment and an antique truck.

At 1.3 miles a trail to the right (west) heads out to the park road; stay left (south) to continue on the loop. A cou-ple hundred feet past this trail you will pass the outlet from the east-west cutoff trail on your left (east). The next trail on the right (west) takes you back to the trailhead.

Miles and Directions

0.0 Start from the trailhead in picnic area #4.

0.3 Take the trail to the right (south) at the juncture with the cutoff trail.

0.6 Pass along the edges of some backyards.

0.7 Continue on the trail to the right (north) at the juncture with the cutoff trail.

1.3 Pass the spur trail to the park road on your right (west).

1.4 Arrive back at the trailhead on the right (west).

11 Fox River Park: Green Trail

The scenic Fox River runs along one side of this wood-and-wetlands park in Waukesha. The trail rolls with the land making this more than a stroll, and observation points will satisfy those looking for wildlife, especially waterfowl.

Distance: 1.6-mile loop
Approximate hiking time: 45 minutes
Difficulty: Easy to moderate for some steepness
Trail surface: Wood chips, asphalt on bike path
Best seasons: Year-round
Other trail users: None
Canine compatibility: Leashed dogs permitted; you are required to pick up after your pet

Fees and permits: A daily entrance fee is charged or a yearly vehicle sticker is required.
Schedule: Open from sunrise to 10 p.m. year-round
Maps: USGS Genesee; a map board is at the trailhead
Trail contact: Fox River Park, W264 S4500 River Rd., Waukesha 53189; (262) 970-6690; www.waukeshacountyparks.com

Finding the trailhead: From I-94 west take WI 164 south. South of Waukesha, Highways 164 and 59 (which have merged by this point) diverge. Continue straight on WI 59 (Les Paul Parkway). Go left (south) on Saylesville Road and then left (west) on CR H. The park entrance is on the left (north) side of the road just after you cross the Fox River. From the park entrance take the first left (heading north) into the family picnic area. Walk past the gate at the end of the lot and turn right (northeast) on the paved bike path into the woods. A map board with a map box marks the trailhead. Trailhead facilities include restrooms, water, and picnic areas. GPS: N42 57.80' / W88 16.46'

The Hike

The Fox River passes through Waukesha on its journey to the Gulf of Mexico via the Mississippi. This hike, in contrast, is a much shorter journey, but its up-and-down terrain puts a little bit of work into it. The hiking trails are color-coded blue, red, and green. All of them are packed to facilitate hiking, snowshoeing and cross-country skiing in the winter. The route described here follows the green trail. An easier alternative to the colored trails is the park's 2.25-mile double-loop paved bike path, which is unshaded and level and also maintained in winter to facilitate hiking.

From the family picnic area parking lot, enter the woods on the bike path and head toward the maps and map board at the trailhead. The asphalt path connects to the City of Waukesha's Fox River Trail, which is shared with bicycles. About 100 feet along the paved path step off to the right (northeast) on the wood-chip trail. At the next four-way juncture, a trail leads out to the picnic area to the right (south) and the return path is coming from your left (north). Just keep straight through here on the green trail.

The path shows short moderate climbs and descents. At the next four-way intersection take the path to the right (south) to stay on the green trail. The path straight ahead is the red trail, and to the left (north) is the blue, both of which connect again into the green trail in other areas of the park and could function as alternative routes.

The green trail continues under open sky, and crosses the bike path and park road at 0.4 mile. The trail goes all the way around the park but you have the options to shorten the route, first with the red trail (the next trail intersection on your left [west]), or the blue trail (the next junction on

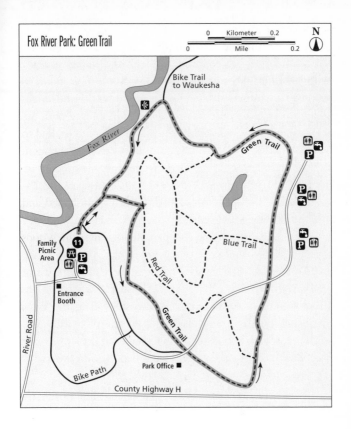

0 Kilometer 0.2

0 Mile 0.2

N

Bike Trail
to Waukesha

Fox River

Green Trail

Family
Picnic
Area

11

Blue Trail

Red Trail

Green Trail

Entrance
Booth

River Road

Bike Path

Park Office ■

County Highway H

your left [west] after you cross the park road once more). If
you always stay with the right-leading path you will remain
on the green trail, which loops through the north end of the
park and comes back to the riverside. It follows the river,
parallel to the bike path, back to the trailhead, passing an
observation point along the way.

Along the blue path, which shows some steep climbs,
you will also find an observation platform overlooking the

park's pond and ephemeral marsh. A connector trail short-ens the blue trail and another connects it to the green trail.

Miles and Directions

0.0 Start by following the paved path to the right (north).

0.1 At the first trail juncture go straight (east) on the green trail.

0.4 Cross the park road.

0.7 Cross the park road again.

0.8 Meet the blue trail.

1.4 Come to the riverside observation point.

1.6 Arrive back at the trailhead.

12 Scuppernong Trails

A scenic overlook gives a view for miles, and rolling hills through pine forest will invigorate the spirit. Popular with joggers, these trails offer three levels of difficulty all dependent on inclines.

Distance: 5.4-mile loop

Approximate hiking time: 1.5 to 2 hours

Difficulty: Moderate due to some steep portions

Trail surface: Packed dirt, crushed rock, some grass

Best seasons: Spring, summer, fall

Other trail users: Foot traffic only; cross-country skiers in winter

Canine compatibility: Leashed dogs permitted

Fees and permits: State park vehicle fee required

Schedule: Open daily from 6 a.m. to 11 p.m.

Maps: USGS Eagle; map boards at trail junctions and maps at the small park booth in the parking lot

Trail contact: Southern Unit Kettle Moraine State Forest Headquarters, S91 W39091 WI 59, Eagle 53119; (262) 594-6200; dnr.wi.gov/org/land/parks/specific/kms

Special considerations: No hiking or dogs are allowed when snow is present. Parts of the park are open to hunters with guns during deer-hunting season at the end of November.

Finding the trailhead: From Milwaukee take I-94 west toward Madison. Get off at exit 282 and take WI 67 left (south) to CR ZZ. You will pass CR ZZ westbound on the right and continue another 0.3 mile to take CR ZZ on the left, going east. The park entrance is 0.4 mile on the left (northwest). The trailhead is at the north corner of the lot. Restrooms and water are available. GPS: N42 56.45' / W88 27.70'

The Hike

Not to be confused with Scuppernong Springs Nature Trail, this collection of three forest loops passes across higher ground than its neighbor. Also, unlike the springs trail, this area has pit toilets and drinking water. The trail doubles as a cross-country ski trail, and the short climbs up and over the roller-coaster terrain make this popular also for cross-country runners.

Colored map boards are located at each trail juncture. The Green Loop is the outermost of the three color-coded trails. The Red Loop is the easiest of the three, getting you back to the trailhead in 2.3 miles; the Orange Loop makes it a 4.2-mile hike. The longer Green Loop is described here.

The trail from the parking lot bears left (northwest) into the woods, passing a park service road. At the first juncture, just 150 feet in, take the path to the right (northeast), a somewhat sandy and pine-needle strewn lane. At the juncture at 0.7 mile, a hard right will take you to D. J. Mackie group picnic area where you can find water near the parking lot. The Red Loop is to the left. The Green and Orange Loops follow the trail that bends a bit to the right (east).

At 1.5 mile you will cross the Ice Age National Scenic Trail, which passes through this park on its 1,000-mile-plus journey across Wisconsin. This trail is marked with yellow blazes on trees and trail posts. Continue to the right (northeast) on the wider path.

At 2.3 miles the Orange Loop leaves this path to the left (south). You'll cross the Ice Age Trail again at 3.1 miles. At 3.5 miles the Red and Orange Loops rejoin the Green trail from the left (southeast). The 0.4-mile lollipop Observation Loop is another 300 feet farther on your right (north), with a scenic overlook at the far end of it.

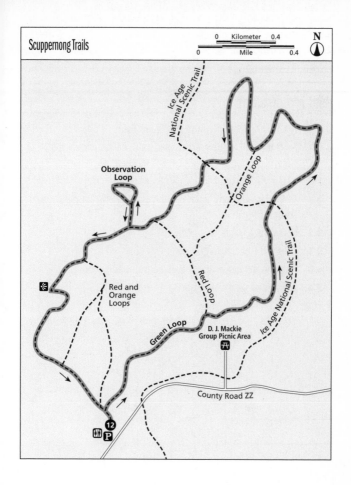

0   Kilometer   0.4

0   Mile   0.4

N

Ice Age National Scenic Trail

Orange Loop

Observation Loop

Red Loop

Red and Orange Loops

Green Loop

Ice Age National Scenic Trail

D. J. Mackie Group Picnic Area

County Road ZZ

12
P

Returning from the overlook, continue right (southwest) on the Green Loop. At the next intersection, the Red and Orange Loops go straight (south). The Green Loop is the path to the right (southwest), and this section is the most challenging, climbing to an overlook at 4.6 miles. The Red and Orange Loops split as they head south, and you will pass them both on your left (north) as the Green Loop returns to the trailhead.

Miles and Directions

0.0   Start by heading north on the Green Loop.

0.7   Pass the trail to the group picnic area, continuing on the Green Loop.

1.5   Cross the Ice Age Trail.

2.3   At the Orange Loop juncture, stay right (north) on the Green Loop.

3.1   Cross the Ice Age Trail again.

3.5   Take the Observation Loop.

4.6   Check out the scenic overlook on the Green Loop.

5.4   Arrive back at the trailhead.

13 Scuppernong Springs Nature Trail

Follow a self-guided nature trail through woods full of springs and patches of scenic wetland. The nature trail booklet has more to say about the human history of this spot.

Distance: 1.5-mile loop
Approximate hiking time: 45 minutes
Difficulty: Easy to moderate when muddy
Trail surface: Packed dirt, sand, and boardwalks
Best seasons: Spring, summer, fall
Other trail users: None
Canine compatibility: Dogs not permitted
Fees and permits: State park vehicle fee required

Schedule: Open daily from 6 a.m. to 11 p.m.
Maps: USGS Eagle
Trail contact: Southern Unit Kettle Moraine State Forest Headquarters, S91 W39091 WI 59, Eagle 53119; (262) 594-6200; dnr.wi.gov/org/land/parks/specific/kms
Special considerations: Mosquitoes can be a nuisance in season, as can soggy trails. The parking lot is plowed in winter.

Finding the trailhead: From Milwaukee take I-94 west toward Madison. Get off at exit 282 and take WI 67 left (south) to CR ZZ. Go right (east) on CR ZZ. The parking lot is on the left (east), opposite the entrance to the Ottawa Lake Recreation Area. Find the trailhead at the east end of the parking lot. Restrooms and water are available across the road at the Ottawa Lake Recreation Center. GPS: N42 56.14' / W88 28.45'

The Hike

Scuppernong means "sweet-scented land" in the native Ho-Chunk language. Native Americans occupied this site, no

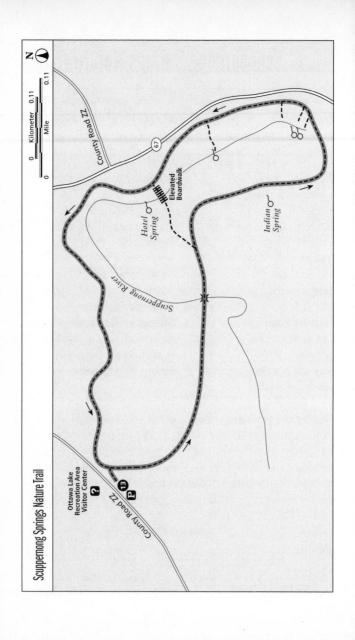

Scuppernong Springs Nature Trail

doubt, for its abundant fresh water. A booklet, available at the trailhead, guides you past numbered posts along the trail and narrates a bit of cultural history.

Just inside the woods from the trailhead the trail forks and you take the path to the right (south). Much of the trail is shaded but with the abundance of springs and low spots you can expect some mud to contend with.

At 0.2 mile you will encounter railroad ties, part of an old railroad bed that extends about 300 feet along the trail. About 200 feet later you will find a concrete wall from the old marl works. (Marl is a lime-rich soil used for mortar and as fertilizer.) A spur trail walks right around it and back onto the main trail.

At 0.3 mile you will cross a bridge over the Scuppernong River, and then the trail becomes a little sandy as it climbs gently to higher ground. Three hundred feet later the trail forks again. To the left (northeast) is a cutoff trail to the return path of the loop. Take the path to the right (east, then south) and enter a bit of prairie where you will likely find abundant wildflowers.

A spur trail to the right (southwest) at signpost #6 leads down the hill into an unmaintained path through brush to the edge of a spring creek. Continuing on the main trail another 200 feet you come to a steep spur trail down to the right to a wooden platform overlooking Indian Spring. Staying on the main trail, head downhill and pass a park maintenance road on the right (southwest) as the trail begins to curve east.

At 0.7 mile you'll pass a concrete wall just above the springs. The trail curves north and passes boardwalk spur trails into the marshy spring area to the left (west). At 0.8 mile a long straight boardwalk heads left (west) out into the spring area. The other end of the cutoff trail is at 0.9 mile, and if you go left onto it you will get a nice view of the water from a boardwalk bridge.

Hotel Spring is just north of the bridge. Continue on the main trail, passing a spur trail on the right that heads up out of the park to the nearby highway. Stay straight (west) on a series of boardwalks, and the trail meanders through the woods back to the trailhead.

Miles and Directions

0.0 Start in the woods, taking the path right (south) at the trail fork.

0.3 Cross the river.

0.7 Reach the concrete wall and the springs.

0.9 Pass the elevated boardwalk and cutoff trail.

1.5 Arrive back at the trailhead.

14 Lapham Peak Park/Kettle Moraine State Forest: Kame Terrace Trail

Hike over glacial terrain amid hardwood forests on this section of an extensive trail system in the Kettle Moraine State Forest. Don't miss the Butterfly Garden at the center of the loop, and the 45-foot observation tower in the middle of the park.

Distance: 2-mile loop

Approximate hiking time: 45 minutes to 1 hour

Difficulty: Moderate due to some short climbs

Trail surface: Grass, packed dirt

Best seasons: Spring, summer, fall

Other trail users: Foot traffic only; skiers in winter

Canine compatibility: Leashed dogs permitted

Fees and permits: State park vehicle fee required

Schedule: Open daily from 7 a.m. to 9 p.m. (until 10 p.m. in winter)

Maps: USGS Oconomowoc East; map board at the trailhead; map available online at www.dnr.state .wi.us/org/land/parks/specific/ lapham/Laphammap.pdf

Trail contacts: Kettle Moraine State Forest—Lapham Peak Unit, W329 N846 CR C, Delafield 53018; (262) 646-3025 (office); (262) 646-4421 (trail information); www.dnr.state.wi .us/org/land/parks/specific/ lapham; www.laphampeak friends.org

Other: Hiking is not allowed when snow is present. This is part of a much larger trail system with more challenging hikes. A 1.5-mile paved accessible trail also starts near the map board. Be sure to visit the Observation Tower at the center of the park before or after your hike.

Finding the trailhead: Go west on I-94 to exit 285 for CR C. The exit ramp curves back in the direction you came from, so turn right (south) on CR C and drive 0.8 mile to the park entrance on the left (east). Take the park road 0.7 mile to the Homestead Hollow parking area on the left (north). The trailhead is to the right of the restrooms, where you will also see a trail map kiosk. GPS: N43 02.38' / W88 23.56'

The Hike

Lapham Peak is named for Wisconsin's first great scientist and naturalist, Increase Lapham. The "peak" is a glacial formation known as a kame. Meltwater flowed straight down a hole in the 1-mile-thick ice sheet, carrying debris and depositing it in a cone shape. The kame terrace then was created by a large glacial river flowing past the kame.

Within the park's 1,000 acres is some fascinating and rugged topography, and there are over 17 miles of trails to explore. Plus, the Ice Age National Scenic Trail passes through the park. All trails are marked with color-coded symbols; the wavy purple one that resembles the Pepsi logo marks the gentler Kame Terrace Trail.

The trail follows a wide mowed path up the hill behind the map board. When it meets the woods you will face a very steep but short climb to the top of the hill. You can bypass this climb by taking the paved accessible Plantation Path, which climbs more gently, and then use a connecting path to rejoin the purple trail.

At 0.3 mile a juncture shows the connecting trail to the right (west), and a cutoff trail through a meadow to the left (east). Here you will also find the Butterfly Garden. Keep straight (south) past this juncture. At a fork in the trail at 0.5 mile, you will take the left (southeast) path. (The more

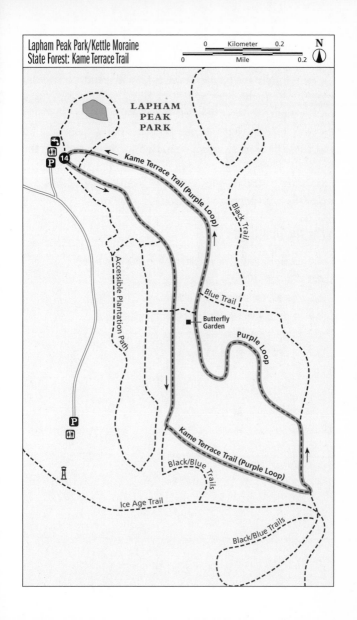

Lapham Peak Park/Kettle Moraine
State Forest: Kame Terrace Trail

0   Kilometer   0.2

0   Mile   0.2

N

LAPHAM
PEAK
PARK

14

Kame Terrace Trail (Purple Loop)

Black Trail

Accessible Plantation Path

Blue Trail

Butterfly
Garden

Purple Loop

Kame Terrace Trail (Purple Loop)

Black/Blue Trails

Ice Age Trail

Black/Blue Trails

challenging black and blue trails follow the path to the right [south].)

At 0.8 mile the Kame Terrace Trail descends to another juncture with the blue and black trails, which come back on the right (south). Stay left (northwest), and at the next juncture take the left (northwest) path. You'll descend a bit and come back up to the open meadow, passing through the Butterfly Garden and crossing a previous juncture. On the other side of the meadow the trail reenters the woods and makes its way down to the trailhead once more.

Miles and Directions

0.0 Start by taking the purple trail from the map board.

0.3 Pass the Butterfly Garden.

0.5 Go left (southeast) at the fork.

0.8 Meet and briefly join the black and blue trails.

1.2 Pass the Butterfly Garden once again.

2.0 Arrive back at the trailhead.

15 Lapham Peak Park/Kettle Moraine State Forest: Meadow Trail

Just as much meadow as it is forest, this trail gives a taste of what you might find at the venerable Lapham Peak Park and shows signs of Native American culture—the unusually bent marker trees are believed to indicate trails or water sources.

Distance: 2-mile loop

Approximate hiking time: 45 minutes to 1 hour

Difficulty: Easy with some moderate climbs

Trail surface: Grass

Best seasons: Spring, summer, fall

Other trail users: Foot traffic only; skiers in winter

Canine compatibility: Leashed dogs permitted

Fees and permits: State park vehicle fee required

Schedule: Open daily from 7 a.m. to 9 p.m. (until 10 p.m. in winter)

Maps: USGS Oconomowoc East; map available online at www.dnr .state.wi.us/org/land/parks/ specific/lapham/Laphammap.pdf

Trail contacts: Kettle Moraine State Forest—Lapham Peak Unit, W329 N846 CR C, Delafield 53018; (262) 646-3025 (office), (262) 646-4421 (trail information); www.dnr.state.wi .us/org/land/parks/specific/ lapham; www.laphampeak friends.org

Other: Trails are closed to hiking when snow is present. This is part of a much larger trail system with more challenging hikes. Be sure to visit the Observation Tower at the center of the park before or after your hike.

Finding the trailhead: Go west from Milwaukee on I-94 to exit 285 for CR C. The exit ramp curves back in the direction you came from, so turn right (south) on CR C and drive 0.8 mile to the park entrance on the left (east). At the first intersection past the park office, take a right (south) turn into the Evergreen Grove parking area. The trailhead is on the left (east) as you enter the lot. Restrooms and water are available at the trailhead. GPS: N43 02.43' / W88 24.16'

The Hike

Lapham Peak is a regular hiking mecca. Trails are color-coded and can be mixed and matched. The park signage clearly shows the colors, as do the trail maps that even list step-by-step trail difficulty if you want to avoid the leg burners. The two trails included in this guide tend toward the easy side, and the Meadow Trail is coded green.

From the trailhead enter the meadow and take the trail going right (south). At 0.2 mile the trail goes slightly uphill, out of the open meadow, passing a cutoff trail on the left (north) that would shorten the loop by more than half. Go right (east, then south) along the trees and the trail will bring you back out into open meadow with scattered clumps of trees.

At 0.5 mile the Ice Age National Scenic Trail, a rustic footpath marked with yellow blazes on posts and trees, crosses your path. The Meadow Trail bends left and heads south just inside the park boundary, along CR C, until it turns left (northeast) at a trail juncture. The much longer (and more difficult) black and blue trails continue straight ahead (southeast). Stay on the green trail.

In 0.1 mile, the trail descends to another intersection with the black and blue trails coming from the southeast. Join them and continue downhill. Once again you cross the Ice Age Trail, at the 1.1-mile mark. Taken to the right (east) the Ice Age Trail would lead you on a rugged path uphill to the 45-foot observation tower on top of Waukesha

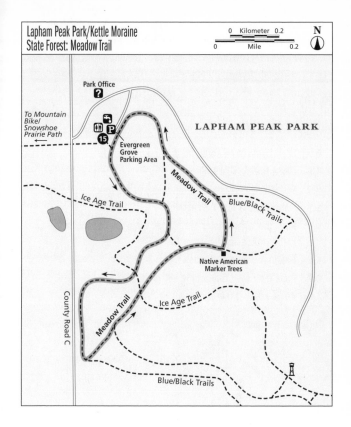

To Mountain
Bike/
Snowshoe
Prairie Path

County's highest point. This side trip would be about 0.6 mile one way and negotiate almost a 250-foot change in altitude.

Continuing from the Ice Age Trail crossing, you'll come to another cutoff trail at 1.2 miles. Stay right (east). At 1.3 miles look for Native American marker trees (bent as saplings to mark trails), and the accompanying storyboard. Go left (north) at the juncture nearby; going straight (east) will bring you to two steep climbs on the black and blue trails before they loop around and rejoin the green trail.

Going left (northeast) at the next juncture, the green, black, and blue trails descend to the meadow area once again and loop around to the trailhead.

Miles and Directions

0.0 Start by heading south on the green trail.

0.5 Cross the Ice Age Trail.

0.9 Take the green trail left (northeast) at the fork.

1.1 Cross the Ice Age Trail again.

1.4 Pass the Native American marker trees and stay with the green trail, going left (north).

1.5 Rejoin the blue and black trails.

1.7 Pass the cutoff trail on the left (south).

2.0 Arrive back at the trailhead.

16 Nashotah Park: Green Trail

The variety of landscapes in this park—including marshland, lakes, and hardwood forest—offers great habitat for birds and other wildlife, and the rolling terrain gives you scenic overlooks of the water and a little extra exercise.

Distance: 3.4-mile loop

Approximate hiking time: 1.5 to 2 hours

Difficulty: Easy to moderate due to some steepness

Trail surface: Grass, wood chips, packed dirt

Best seasons: Spring, summer, fall

Other trail users: None

Canine compatibility: Leashed dogs permitted; owners are required to pick up after their pets

Fees and permits: A daily entrance fee is charged or a yearly vehicle sticker is required.

Schedule: Open from sunrise to 10 p.m. year-round

Maps: USGS Oconomowoc East; map boards at the trailhead and along the route; park map available online at www .waukeshacounty.gov/page.aspx? SetupMetaId=11024&id=11220

Trail contact: Nashotah Park, W330 N5113 CR C, Nashotah 53058; (262) 367-1022; www .waukeshacountyparks.com

Finding the trailhead: From Milwaukee follow I-94 west, just past downtown Delafield, and take the CR C exit (exit 285). Follow CR C north 4 miles to the park entrance on the left (west). Drive to picnic area #2. The trailhead is down the hill toward the woods, behind the pavilion. Water and restrooms are at the picnic area. GPS: N43 06.68' / W88 24.54'

The Hike

For a park of 443 acres, Nashotah has quite a variety of habitats. With lakes, wetlands, savanna, meadows, cedar glades, and hardwood forest, the park is home to a variety of plants and animals, in particular songbirds.

There is a map board at the trailhead, as well as at most trail junctures throughout the hike. To the left (east) of the trailhead is the entrance to the blue trail, an easy 1.5-mile alternative loop along the edge of Forest Lake. The red and green trails start together into the forest, but the red parts to the right (northwest) at the first juncture at 0.2 mile, where there is another map board. The red trail is the most strenuous but extends only 1 mile.

On the green trail, you'll continue south alongside and above Forest Lake, but soon you'll descend to lake level. The trail makes the turn west and at 0.7 mile you'll come to a connector trail. The green trail goes steeply down to the right (north) here. If you prefer to skip the incline stay straight (northwest) and the connector trail reconnects with the green trail not even 0.2 mile later. It's a horse apiece. One horse will be slightly more tired.

You will enter a clearing just before the next juncture. Here the green trail goes straight across, while another trail leads right (northwest) and downhill to the connector trail to the inner red loop. A similar trail comes up at a different angle from the connector trail to the green trail, and you will pass that on the right on the other side of the clearing.

At 1.4 mile you'll see the entrance to the dumbbell-shaped self-guided nature trail on the right (east). The green trail continues north past this, skirting the edge of the park property and showing Grass Lake through the trees to the right (east).

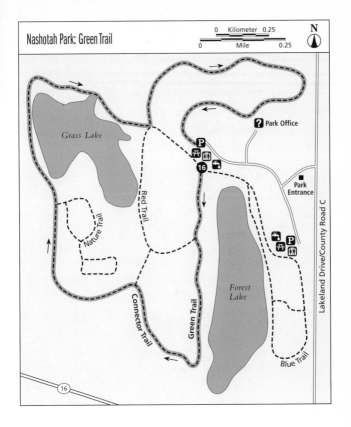

The hike makes the turn east around the top of the lake. At 2.2 miles you'll find the red trail, which can take you back to the picnic area. Otherwise continue left (north, then east) on the green trail, completing the final loop through mostly meadow, and passing the park office on your left (south) before arriving back at the parking lot.

The trails are groomed for skiing in the winter but the park offers alternative trails for hiking or snowshoeing.

Miles and Directions

0.0   Start from the trailhead in picnic area #2.

0.2   Pass the red trail juncture.

1.4   Reach the entrance to the nature trail.

2.2   Arrive at the second red trail juncture.

3.0   Pass the park office.

3.4   Arrive back at the parking lot.

17 Ice Age National Scenic Trail: Monches Segment

This segment of the Ice Age National Scenic Trail passes through the Carl Schurz Forest over glacial moraines, and then descends into wetlands and lowland forest to follow the Oconomowoc River. This hike is even more impressive when fall colors hit their peak.

Distance: 3.2 miles one way (or 6.4 miles out and back)

Approximate hiking time: 1.5 to 2 hours one way

Difficulty: Moderate to difficult due to trail surface and steepness

Trail surface: Packed dirt with roots and rocks; several boardwalks

Best seasons: Year-round, but wet periods can be muddy

Other trail users: None

Canine compatibility: Dogs permitted

Fees and permits: No fees or permits required

Schedule: Open 24 hours daily

Maps: USGS Merton; Ice Age Trail Atlas

Trail contact: Kris Jensen (volunteer), Waukesha/Milwaukee County Chapter, Ice Age Trail, W316 N7351 Nelson Dr., Hartland 53029; (262) 966-9788; krjonorthlk@yahoo.com; www.iceagetrail.org

Finding the trailhead: From Milwaukee take I-94 west to WI 16. Get off WI 16 in Hartland at exit 183, and go straight (west), across Merton Avenue on Hartbrook Drive (parallel to WI 16), to North Avenue/CR E. Take this right (north) and remain on CR E for 4 miles, all the way through Monches to where it intersects with CR K and CR Q. Turn left (west) on CR Q and the trailhead is immediately on the left (south). (The southern trailhead and parking lot are 0.3 mile to the west of CR E on Funk Road, 2.6 miles south of Monches.) GPS: N43 11.58' / W88 20.79'

The Hike

The northern portion of this segment of the Ice Age National Scenic Trail travels primarily up and down moraines through the forest dedicated to Wisconsin conservationist Carl Schurz. The southern portion follows the marshy edge of the Oconomowoc River, which drains marshland in the Kettle Moraine area. If you see the yellow blazes on the trees, you are on the official Ice Age Trail. Blue blazes indicate spur trails; unmarked trails lead elsewhere.

Remember, the trail passes over private land. Respect the privilege of its use by staying on the path and leaving nothing behind but footprints. The route is described here as a one-way trek, from north to south, with a pickup at the south end. But it can be done as an out-and-back trek. The trail is mostly shaded and uneven with rocks and tree roots. Mosquitoes can be more of an issue closer to the river. Footbridge planks can be as slippery as ice when wet.

Starting from the northern trailhead, the trail heads immediately uphill. At 0.3 mile be careful to duck a wire across the trail about 5 feet off the ground; this is to keep horses off the path. A memorial boulder is just beyond.

At the juncture at 1.1 miles, go left (southeast) at the bench and watch for yellow blazes. The trail comes to the river at 1.5 miles and passes through a narrow stretch of trees and brush between river on the left (east) and farmland on the right (west). One-tenth of a mile later, you'll cross the river on a bridge and some boardwalks with tree roots between them. Take care.

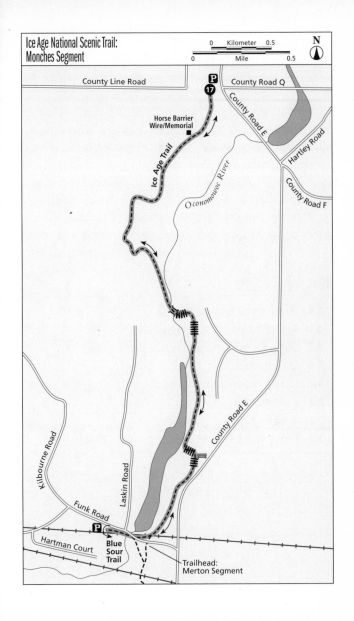

Ice Age National Scenic Trail:
Monches Segment

0   Kilometer   0.5

0   Mile   0.5

N

County Line Road

County Road Q

P
17

County Road E

Hartley Road

Horse Barrier
Wire/Memorial

Ice Age Trail

Oconomowoc River

County Road F

County Road E

Kilbourne Road

Laskin Road

Funk Road

P

Hartman Court

Blue
Sour
Trail

Trailhead:
Merton Segment

The trail moves away from the river on the other side. At the next juncture follow the trail marker to the right (south). Cross a boardwalk over a soggy low spot at 1.8 miles and the trail goes close to the river once more. The route ventures into the open as it bends west and travels under power lines, then it comes out on a crushed limestone path to Funk Road. To the left (south) is the railroad viaduct. Take Funk Road to the right (west) and cross the river. On the left side of the road is the short blue segment of the trail that takes you to the Ice Age Trail parking lot.

This segment connects to the Loew Lake and Merton Segments of the Ice Age Trail, to the north and south respectively.

Miles and Directions

0.0 Start from the northern trailhead.

0.3 Pass under a horse barrier wire.

1.1 Follow the trail to the left (southeast) of the bench.

1.6 Cross the river.

1.8 Use the boardwalk to cross mud.

2.7 Cross a brook.

3.1 Cross Funk Road.

3.2 End at the Ice Age Trail parking lot on Funk Road.

18 Ice Age National Scenic Trail: Southern Holy Hill Segment

Hike a portion of the Ice Age National Scenic Trail as it passes through forest and prairie over moraines and kames. Then have a look at the Holy Hill Basilica on top of a 1,335-foot kame. From the top you can see all the way to Milwaukee.

Distance: 5.6 miles out and back

Approximate hiking time: 2.5 to 3 hours

Difficulty: Moderate to difficult due to steepness and trail surface

Trail surface: Packed dirt with tree roots and loose stones; steps and asphalt for the basilica climb

Best seasons: Spring, summer, fall

Other trail users: None

Canine compatibility: Dogs permitted on the Ice Age Trail, but not on the basilica climb

Fees and permits: No fees or permits required for the Ice Age Trail; a fee is required to enter the basilica

Schedule: Open 24 hours daily

Maps: USGS Merton; Ice Age Trail Atlas

Trail contacts: Ice Age Trail Alliance, Washington/Ozaukee County Chapter, 2110 Main St., Cross Plains 53528; (800) 227-0046; www.iceagetrail.org. Basilica of Holy Hill; www.holyhill.com

Special considerations: The basilica grounds close at 5 p.m. daily.

Finding the trailhead: From Milwaukee take I-94 west, exiting onto WI 16 west. At Hartland take exit 181 for WI 83 North. Follow WI 83 north through Hartland to WI 167/Holy Hill Road, and turn right (east). At Station Way Road (past the Holy Hill entrance) take a right (heading south), and at about 0.2 mile you'll find the parking lot on your left (east). The trailhead is on the left (north) as you enter the parking lot. The northbound trailhead is across Station Way Road from the lot. There are restrooms in the basilica visitor center. GPS: N43 14.90' / W88 19.53'

Parking at the south trail endpoint of this segment is not permitted, but there is a small parking lot on Shannon Road just west of the northernmost trailhead. Additional options include parking next to the trailhead on the north side of Holy Hill Road/WI 167, or in the lot at St. Mary's Chapel (which closes at 5 p.m.).

The Hike

A national Shrine of Mary, Holy Hill Basilica is built atop a glacial formation called a kame, formed by debris deposited by a stream that once rushed straight down through the thick sheet of ice above. This segment of the Ice Age Trail approaches from the north, passes around the kame, and heads south.

The best option for hiking this segment is to park in the middle of the hike on Station Way Road and hike the northern and southern halves each as out-and-back routes. The trailhead is marked at the head of the southern half, the harder of the two halves. The trail makes some strenuous climbs and descents over smaller kames and moraines as it weaves its way through the forest, offering at least one good view of the basilica through the branches. Watch the trees for yellow blazes, which designate the official path. Blue blazes mark spur trails that are worth exploring. The trail ends at Donegal Road, and an on-road path to the east connects it to the next segment of the national trail.

The northbound half of this trail starts across Station Way Road. The narrow footpath passes through open woods, with milder inclines than those to the south, crossing Carmel

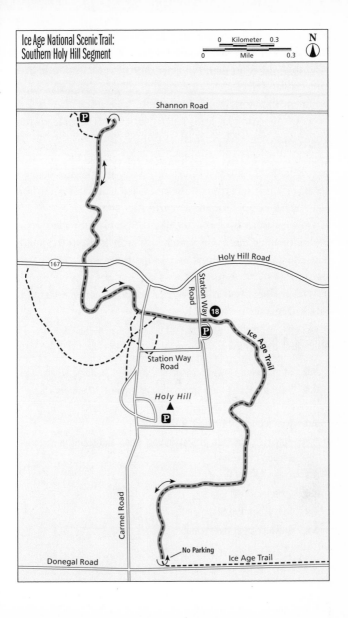

Ice Age National Scenic Trail:
Southern Holy Hill Segment

0   Kilometer   0.3
0   Mile   0.3

N

Shannon Road

P

Holy Hill Road

167

Station Way Road

18

P

Ice Age Trail

Station Way Road

Holy Hill ▲

P

Carmel Road

No Parking

Ice Age Trail

Donegal Road

Road at 0.2 mile and continuing through the forest another 0.5 mile to Holy Hill Road. Directly across (north of) the road the trail continues, this time through more open prairie and brush. The path continues 0.6 mile to the turnaround point at Shannon Road. Just before you reach that point, however, a spur trail leads left (west) about 0.1 mile to the Shannon Road parking lot.

The blue spur trail to the St. Mary's parking lot will connect you to the Erratic Spur, an option that climbs steeply about 0.1 mile to a tremendous view from atop a kame. The huge erratic boulder here is worth the climb alone.

A very short option is to hike the Stations of the Cross. Plenty of steps and some stretches of asphalt climb the kame past the fourteen stations to the basilica above. A visit to the top of the structure incurs a fee but the view is worth it. The basilica itself is one of the most important Christian pilgrimage sites in the Midwest.

Miles and Directions

0.0 Start from trailhead on Station Way Road, heading south.

0.4 Pass the Kame View Trail on the right (west). Continue south on the Ice Age Trail.

1.4 Turn around at Donegal Road.

2.8 Return to trailhead at Station Way Road and start the north section of the trail.

3.1 Cross Carmel Road.

3.5 Cross Holy Hill Road.

4.2 Turn around at Shannon Road.

5.6 Arrive back at the trailhead.

19 Harrington Beach State Park

An often overlooked state park not far from the city, Harrington Beach offers the beauty of a 1-mile, undeveloped, sandy beach on the shores of Lake Michigan, a quarry lake, cedar lowland forest, and historical landmarks from an old mining community.

Distance: 3-mile circuit

Approximate hiking time: 2 hours

Difficulty: Easy, with avoidable sections rated moderate due to trail surface

Trail surface: Mostly paved or crushed stone; some uneven packed dirt paths

Best seasons: Spring, summer, fall

Other trail users: Bicyclists; park shuttle

Canine compatibility: Leashed dogs permitted but not on the nature trail

Fees and permits: State park vehicle fee required

Schedule: Open daily from 6 a.m. to 11 p.m.

Maps: USGS Port Washington East; park map available at the park welcome center and online at www.dnr.state.wi.us/Org/land/parks/specific/harrington/pdfs/hbmap.pdf

Trail contact: Harrington Beach State Park, 531 CR D, Belgium 53004; (262) 285-3015; www.dnr.state.wi.us/Org/land/parks/specific/harrington

Finding the trailhead: From Milwaukee take I-43 north for 35 miles to exit 107, and turn right (west) on CR D. Follow CR D for 1.2 miles to the park entrance on the right (south). Follow the park road for 1.5 miles to the Ansay Welcome Center. The trailhead is to the left (east) of the building. Restrooms and water are available at the park welcome center. GPS: N43 29.81' / W87 47.67'

The Hike

In addition to a sandy beach and cool lake breezes, Harrington Beach State Park offers a great shaded hike. To the right (west) side of the Ansay Welcome Center is the paved shuttle trail, on which only the free shuttle circles the park until 7 p.m. The hike as marked, however, begins to the left (east) of the welcome center. Only 200 feet into mixed forest from the trailhead, steps lead off the trail to the left (east), down to the beach, which stretches south from here for nearly 1 mile.

Continuing on the trail from the top of the steps, hike southward through the forest not far from the edge of the beach, passing occasional benches and spur trails out onto the sand. At 0.3 mile the trail joins the shuttle path to the left (west). Watch for various signs indicating ruins of an old mining community.

Just 100 feet down the shuttle path, take a paved path to the right (west) to Quarry Lake for a 0.7-mile loop. You can cut this out of your park tour for length, but it is quite scenic. Start the loop to the left (south) and cross a footbridge. The crushed stone path follows the water's edge and passes a few outgoing spur trails. You'll cross another footbridge, and halfway around the lake you will come to a fork in the trail. The path to the right is a spur trail to a lookout point. Take the trail to the left to continue, and just keep going right at trail junctions until you return to the shuttle path and bridge.

Continue to the right (south) on the shuttle path. The trail remains on this paved surface until the 2.2-mile mark. If you prefer the asphalt, stay on it and follow the shuttle path to the park road for a loop back to the parking lot.

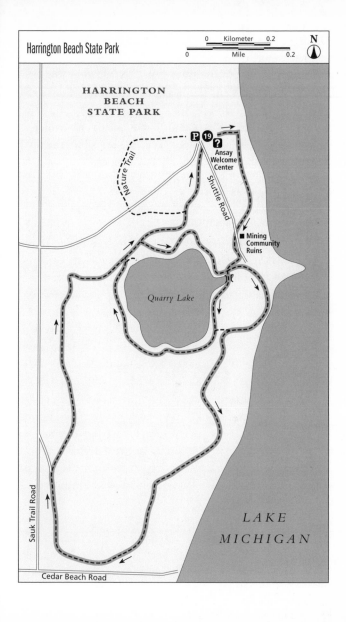

Harrington Beach State Park

HARRINGTON
BEACH
STATE PARK

Nature Trail

P 19 ?
Ansay
Welcome
Center

Shuttle Road

Mining
Community
Ruins

Quarry Lake

Sauk Trail Road

Cedar Beach Road

LAKE
MICHIGAN

Otherwise, leave the pavement for a rugged wooded trail that heads north to a T juncture at 2.6 miles.

Take the path to the right (east), which soon joins the lakeside path again. At the next juncture you will take the path to the left (northeast), back to the parking lot via cedar lowlands. You will pass a trail to the left (west), which is part of the optional nature trail. Take the branch to the right (north) to finish in the parking lot at 3 miles.

Miles and Directions

0.0 Start from the Ansay Welcome Center.

0.3 Take the Quarry Lake loop.

1.2 Return to the shuttle path.

2.2 Take the wooded trail from the shuttle path.

3.0 Arrive back at the parking lot.

20 Kohler-Andrae State Park: Dunes Cordwalk

Set along a beautiful sandy beach on Lake Michigan, this state park protects a fragile ecosystem set among sand dunes. A cordwalk traverses the grass-covered rolling sands and offers views of the lake and rare plant species.

Distance: 2.8 miles out and back

Approximate hiking time: 1.5 to 2 hours

Difficulty: Moderate due to trail surface and some steepness

Trail surface: Cordwalk with some sandy patches; can be slippery

Best seasons: Year-round, except when snow and ice are present

Other trail users: None

Canine compatibility: Dogs permitted on leashes, but not on the Creeping Juniper Nature Trail or on the beach south of the Sanderling Nature Center

Fees and permits: State park vehicle fee required

Schedule: Open daily from 6 a.m. to 11 p.m.

Maps: USGS Sheboygan South; park map available at the park office or online at www.dnr.state .wi.us/org/land/parks/specific/ ka/maps.htm

Trail contact: Kohler-Andrae State Park; 1020 Beach Park Lane, Sheboygan 53081; (920) 451-4080; www.dnr.state.wi.us/ org/land/parks/specific/ka

Special considerations: Be aware on hot summer days that there is little shade on this trail. Also, this is a state natural area and as such has extra protections for some rare and fragile flora: Stay on the cordwalk at all times.

Finding the trailhead: From Milwaukee take I-43 north 48 miles to exit 120 for CR V. Turn right (northeast) on CR V and in 100 feet turn right (east) again to stay on CR V. Follow CR V for 2 miles to the state park entrance on the right (south), then drive 1.2 miles on Sand Dune Drive to the southern trailhead and parking area for the Dunes Cordwalk. Restrooms and water are available at the trailhead. GPS: N43 39.48' / W87 43.46'

The Hike

The glaciers of the Wisconsin Period of the Ice Age carved out the basin that is now Lake Michigan, depositing fine sand. When the waters of the previous glacial lake receded, beaches emerged and winds created the dunes we see today. The cordwalk, a series of narrow planks that traverses the sands, offers a chance for hikers to responsibly see the fragile dunes and their uncommon plants. The park also has a marshland boardwalk and a woodland trail, parts of which are wheelchair accessible. Just north of the park is a trail system shared with horses.

There are three primary places to enter the cordwalk trail: from the north or south ends, and in the middle. You will find the Sanderling Nature Center, with exhibits about the geology, wildlife, and history of the region, at the middle trailhead. Restrooms can be found inside; otherwise you can find toilets and water in the parking lots at either end of the trail.

Beginning at the southerly trailhead, the cordwalk heads north, rising and falling over the dunes. At 0.1 mile you will pass the trail to the group camp on your left (west). The trail continues around a large cottonwood 300 feet later; this tree, with just a few other clumps of aspen or pine, is the only shade along the trail. Be aware also that sand sometimes drifts over portions of the trail.

The highest points offer great views of the lake to the east, and the layout of the surrounding dunes. At 0.5 mile a

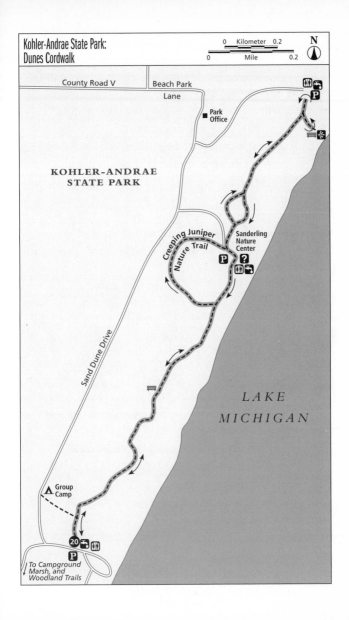

Kohler-Andrae State Park:
Dunes Cordwalk

0   Kilometer   0.2

0   Mile   0.2

N

County Road V

Beach Park
Lane

Park
Office

KOHLER-ANDRAE
STATE PARK

Creeping Juniper
Nature Trail

Sanderling
Nature
Center

Sand Dune Drive

LAKE
MICHIGAN

Group
Camp

20

To Campground
Marsh, and
Woodland Trails

spur trail goes left (west) a short distance into the dunes to a bench in partial shade.

At 0.7 mile take the left (west) branch at the trail fork and you are on the first of two loops embedded in the length of the trail—the Creeping Juniper Nature Trail, which offers some interpretive signage.

At 1 mile you arrive at the parking lot for Sanderling Nature Center. Go left from the trail across the lot's entry to continue the hike north. At the next loop at 1.1 mile take the left (west) branch around to the next juncture and continue north. At 1.4 miles a spur trail goes 150 feet to the right (east) to a bench with a sweeping view of the beach and lake. Just beyond the spur trail is the north parking lot and turnaround point.

The return path follows the second halves of the two loop trails. Always take the left (east) branch, and cross the parking lot past the nature center to find the return path and Creeping Juniper Trail in the corner on the left (southeast).

Miles and Directions

0.0 Start from the south trailhead and head north on the cord-walk.

0.7 Follow Creeping Juniper Nature Trail to the left (west).

1.0 Pass the nature center and parking lot.

1.5 Reach the turnaround point.

2.0 Pass the nature center again.

2.8 Arrive back at the trailhead.

Clubs and Trail Groups

Clubs and trail organizations for hikers are listed below.

- Badger Trails, Inc., P.O. Box 210615, Milwaukee 53221; (414) 777-3920; www.badgertrails.org. Badger Trails is a nonprofit organization promoting hiking in Wisconsin. They sponsor three events each year.

- Ice Age Trail Alliance, 2110 Main St., Cross Plains 53528; (800) 227-0046; www.iceagetrail.org. Though many segments of this national scenic trail have been created, some are still on the way, and the rest are always being maintained. Local chapters organize hikes and trail maintenance events. This is a great bunch of people and a fantastic hiking trail. Check the Web site to find local chapters of the Ice Age Trail Alliance nearest the Milwaukee area.

- Wisconsin Go Hiking Club; (414) 299-9285; wisconsin gohiking.homestead.com. Since its inception in 1924, this club has been promoting outdoor activity. Often there are several hikes each week, in destinations both near and far. Member dues are nominal and event costs are shared by participants.

- MeetUp.com. This social networking group helps you hook up with like-minded locals. Several Milwaukee-area groups have outdoor interests including hiking.

About the Author

Kevin Revolinski has written for the *New York Times* and *Chicago Tribune,* and he is the author of several guidebooks, including *Best Rail Trails Wisconsin* (FalconGuides), *60 Hikes Within 60 Miles Madison, Backroads and Byways of Wisconsin, The Wisconsin Beer Guide: A Travel Companion,* and *The Yogurt Man Cometh: Tales of an American Teacher in Turkey.* He makes base camp in Madison, Wisconsin, and his Web site is www.TheMadTravelerOnline.com.

WHAT'S SO SPECIAL ABOUT UNSPOILED, NATURAL PLACES?

Beauty   Solitude   Wildness   Freedom   Quiet   Adventure
Serenity   Inspiration   Wonder   Excitement
Relaxation   Challenge

There's a lot to love about our treasured public lands, and the reasons are different for each of us. Whatever your reasons are, the national **Leave No Trace** education program will help you discover special outdoor places, enjoy them, and preserve them—today and for those who follow. By practicing and passing along these simple principles, you can help protect the special places you love from being loved to death.

THE PRINCIPLES OF **LEAVE NO TRACE**

- Plan ahead and prepare
- Travel and camp on durable surfaces
- Dispose of waste properly
- Leave what you find
- Minimize campfire impacts
- Respect wildlife
- Be considerate of other visitors

Leave No Trace is a national nonprofit organization dedicated to teaching responsible outdoor recreation skills and ethics to everyone who enjoys spending time outdoors.

To learn more or to become a member, please visit us at www.LNT.org or call (800) 332-4100.

Leave No Trace, P.O. Box 997, Boulder, CO 80306